The ArtSmart Method

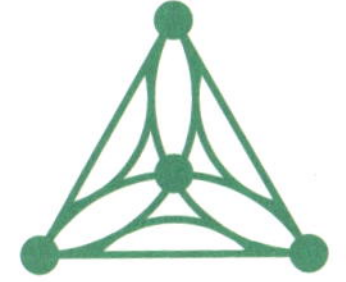

A Guide to Business Autonomy for Artists

Amy Davila

atelier éditions

Contents

Contents

Galleries are neither the problem

nor the
solution for
artists.

Introduction

The Way of ArtSmart

"Be regular and orderly in your life, so that you may be violent and original in your work."—Gustave Flaubert

You might have picked up this book because you're struggling to make your art practice work the way you want it to. Maybe you're tired of being in a reactive position when it comes to your finances. Maybe you're baffled by a peer having a gallery or brand deal when you don't.

Whether you're a week out of art school or had 20 years of studio life, if you're looking for some insider wisdom about organizing, energizing, and taking your art career to the next level, this book is for you.

I run an art business consultancy firm called ArtSmart. My clients range from new graduates who want to create a budget, to mid-career artists looking to sustain momentum, to art studios, galleries, and organizations that employ dozens of people.

Many of my clients have buried their heads in the sand for years when it comes to their finances, and some have gone bankrupt. They sense the imbalance and want to fix it—whether they're looking to get out of a cycle of boom and bust with selling their art, or are managing substantial incomes for the first time in their lives. I work with them to take control of their current money situation. I also assist with cleaning up debt, so they can move forward instead of living constantly in fear of opening the mail.

I want to offer a couple of things with this book: tools to help you achieve business autonomy as an artist, and an empowered way of thinking about your practice. I want to show you that it's good to take risks in your art, and to help you avoid unnecessary risks in your finances or studio business.

The ArtSmart Method covers the practicalities every artist needs to know. It shows how the day-to-day is connected to larger concerns. And since a method is only as good as its usefulness to the person it serves, we'll explore how you can empower your thinking to get the ArtSmart Method working for you. But before I commence with the big reveal, I'd like to share a bit about myself, so you know where I'm coming from.

How I Got Here, Part 1

I'm not an artist. I'm a self-professed lover of Excel spreadsheets; a foul-mouthed ex-cheerleader from Texas; and a reader of science fiction and Eastern philosophy. I have an MBA with an emphasis on tax accounting, 25 years of experience on the business side of galleries, and a consultancy firm that specializes in bringing peace of mind to our clients. Consider me a business therapist focused on creating autonomy for you, the artist.

My background is in systems and efficiencies. I attended the engineering and business school at the University of Texas in the early 1990s, building data models and tutoring advanced calculus. I built projections for mythical companies, extrapolating years into the future and factoring in numerous variables and potential scenarios. I loved transforming a flood of information into something useful—a traversable flow of possibilities.

At school I'd tried to transfer to art history but business kept pulling me back in. After graduation I was quickly hired by a Big Six accounting firm, first in Houston, then in San Francisco. I created tax projection models for companies like The Gap and Starbucks. I developed a knack for problem-solving, systems development, and financial modeling. I was also bored to tears.

I would often think about the first time I experienced the ascensional force of modern art—in Houston, at the Rothko Chapel. Nothing could compete with the effect that those paintings had on me—I wanted in.

I sought an internship at a nearby art gallery. I pitched a trade: I would help them with budgets, cost projections, and profit and loss analysis, and they would give me the art education I'd never received.

I fell dizzyingly in love with the art world. I quit my well-paid, cushy job and moved to New York, where I landed a gig answering phones at David Zwirner. It was a great place to start.

But it didn't escape me that the gallery world was an absolute train wreck. No business reports, budgeting, or cost projections. Nobody wanted to deal with this tedious stuff. I decided to carve out a niche getting the art world in shape: more streamlined, more focused, more intentional. I started to apply my knowledge and skills from the business world, and I haven't looked back.

Over the next six years working at galleries, I sold art, ran operations, built programs, designed websites, curated shows, wrote press releases. I observed the power dynamics of the artist–gallery relationship. Galleries have their place, no doubt about it, as educators, risk-takers, connectors, tastemakers, and rainmakers. I kept hearing the same refrain from my artist friends: "Being represented by a good gallery is the only way I'm going to be taken seriously. That's just the way it works."

Pattern Recognition

I understood, and still understand, what galleries do for artists and how essential they are. But I started to realize the limitations of the gallery system. There are two main issues. One is the inherent conflict of interests that anyone who's spent time in the art world will recognize: a gallery's primary goal is sales; its secondary goal is looking after its artists' best interests. These priorities don't always align, in fact they often conflict. A common example of this is a gallery being desperate to make a sale at an art fair and offering a deep discount to a collector. Because the artist has to split the discount with the gallery, the artist gets hurt financially and has no recourse once the deal is done.

At best, the gallery–artist dynamic creates a healthy power struggle with push and pull toward long-term goals. At worst, this conflict of interests can lead a gallery to exploit or neglect the artists they're meant to protect.

Galleries are neither the problem nor the solution for artists. I've seen artists get representation by a prestigious gallery then get ripped to shreds by art critics. I've seen artists get their wish of representation by a gallery and not get paid their fair share of sales. I've seen artists get gallery representation only to have their work sold to collectors who flip it at auction, potentially compromising the artist's market value.

Since a Goldilocks environment in which artists can settle, prosper, and thrive isn't the reality, I wanted to figure out how an artist could retain control over their finances, and, by extension, their career.

To recognize a pattern, you have to wait. Artists are fascinating to me because, on the surface, they don't seem to have patterns. But the more I worked with them, the more I thought there must be some kind of order. In the words of Keith Haring: "There is order/structure within all matter, all action, all thought, no matter how unstructured it may appear. Time itself imposes structure."

Over time, I started to understand. I was able to answer the question: What external circumstances does a tempestuous and original mind need to succeed?

An Artist Needs ...

Of course, having a good gallery can be a key component to an artist's success, but it's not the only thing that matters.

Galleries, commercial or otherwise, are the cornerstone of the art market. The art market is speculative, capricious, and ultimately hostile. It can be dangerous to an artist's career. Value is arrived at by a complex set of things—trends, connections, the status quo—that have nothing to do with whether something is "good" or praiseworthy.

So if the art market, which is upheld by the gallery system, isn't something an artist can rely on, to whom or what can they turn? I went back to thinking about the problem. What does an artist need to grow and succeed?

I've come to understand that an artist needs three things to thrive. First, an artist needs support, to be upheld by allies, peers, and mentors who provide new ideas, materials, environments, safe-spaces, love, and a sense of self-worth. Second, an artist needs to earn money making art. Like anyone else, artists want to get paid for what they do; they want opportunity and stability. Third, an artist needs exposure in order to make an impact and find audiences. Artists want their work to be recognized. I started to see the artist's pattern and how the gallery fits into it.

A gallery's job is finding new markets, more eyeballs, sympathetic peers, and loyal collectors for artists and their work. It contextualizes the artist for the media, academics, curators, and other artists. The gallery exchanges the artist's work for money, negotiates deals on the artist's behalf, and, ideally, advances the artist funds when necessary. It exhibits the artist's work strategically and promotes it at fairs and on social media. The gallery has become the holy grail to artists because it promises support, money, and exposure: the three ingredients of success.

Support + Money + Exposure

Throughout this book we'll be discussing how you can be a proactive player in finding support, money, and exposure by establishing business autonomy—whether you have a gallery or not. Support is about your wider network and the company you keep. Money is about resources, funding, and financial opportunities. Exposure is about audience engagement and leaving an impression.

All three impact the scope and trajectory of an artist's career, and all three overlap—a gallery can offer you support and money, for example—but, crucially, these elements exist in tension with each other. Each one is important, but often one or two seem more achievable, while the other feels like a remote possibility. For example, after half a decade of supportive group shows, an artist wishes for the exposure that a solo exhibition would bring. Or, after building a massive following on Instagram, an artist is struggling to monetize their practice. Or, after selling work at a commercial gallery, an artist wishes for a stronger community.

At business school, we learned about the famous "iron

triangle" (aka the triple constraint). It goes like this: if you're making something, ideally you want it to be done fast, cheap, and good. But you can't have all three. Any given project is a balancing act of time, cost, and quality.

If I want something that is good quality quickly, it's going to cost money. I gain quality and speed, but it's expensive. Fast + Good = Expensive. An example of this is the rush fees that are charged to push your print job ahead of others. It costs money to take priority.

If my budget shrinks during a project, but I want to keep the quality high, I have to extend my deadline. Because money is compromised, and I still need good quality, it's going to take longer. Cheap + Good = Slow. An example of this is your print job being put in the queue after the jobs that are having more spent on them. Spending less money usually means waiting.

If my timeline shrinks, but I still want to keep costs low, quality will suffer. I gain speed and lower costs but lose good quality. Cheap + Fast = Poor Quality. An example of this is a rush print job in time for Christmas, with inferior paper because the good stuff is on back order.

The iron triangle of fast, cheap, and good doesn't quite translate to the world of the artist, but the patterned thinking does. Once you start looking at your projects strategically and making decisions based on potential losses and gains, you'll start to see your priorities, your potential, and your power to influence in a different light.

How I Got Here, Part 2

Almost 15 years ago I settled in Los Angeles and opened ArtSmart, a private financial consulting practice for artists and galleries. I adapted business tools to formulate a methodology for artists. The ArtSmart Method can be used by artists independently of any gallery or peer group. It's equal parts workbooking and strategic career counseling. I've helped artists get their studio functioning like a business by establishing a solid foundation to build on. I've also provided consulting and guidance about how to navigate opportunities and pitfalls (and how to distinguish between them).

So here it is, the culmination of 25 years of consulting, guiding, and speaking candidly with artists, galleries, creative businesses, and art nonprofits: the ArtSmart Method. You'll come away with a newfound appreciation for the fundamentals of business and contractual agreements, the seeds for strategic thinking, and the desire to be the master of your own universe.

Support + Money + Exposure = Success

We've established that support, money, and exposure are the key elements of a successful art career. We've also noted that they're unlikely to be available to you all at the same time. In fact, these elements work double-time as the necessary constraints that allow you to make decisions about your art practice—like the components of the iron triangle. Let's call the one we've got here—support, money, and exposure—the ArtSmart Triangle.

The ArtSmart Triangle was developed to address the obstacles that artists regularly confront: lack of confidence or comprehension in how to approach peers, gallerists, and collectors; uncertainty about how to position their work; and anxiety about balancing networking and promoting against studio time. And, of course, making do with limited time and financial resources. I'll introduce the ArtSmart Triangle here, and we'll be returning to it in theory and practice throughout the book.

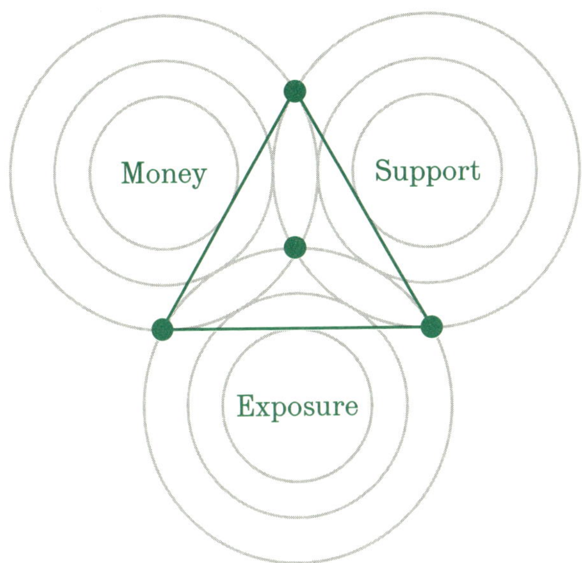

Whenever I need to make a decision, or I'm advising a client on their decision-making, this is where I start: with the goals of support, money, and exposure.

I get my clients to regularly ask themselves these three questions:

- Which goals are available in the scenario?
- Which goals might I have to compromise?
- What, if anything, can I change about the situation to improve my access to these goals?

Here's an example. One of my clients, Jason, was in the middle of completing a major commission for a prominent art collector (*great support*). It was a private commission (*limited exposure*) and we had negotiated a decent artist fee (*good money*). It was a relationship that Jason was eager to foster. However, when he was halfway done with the piece, the collector admitted that, due to the global financial crisis, he could no longer pay the agreed-upon fee. He still wanted the work but was only willing the pay half of the price, or, he threatened, he'd cancel the commission.

We had to assess what Jason could control. When he had accepted the commission, he was going to gain support and money, but circumstances had changed and he risked losing money because the proposed new fee did not cover his time and production costs. If Jason was still gaining support but now sacrificing money, could he do anything about exposure? The market was tanking, galleries were closing, everyone was freaking out. What better time than that moment to ... throw a party? I was half joking when I suggested it, but the idea took root and started to grow.

We got the buyer to agree that, once the commission was completed, a reception would be held to celebrate the patron's collection. The contract allocated some of the funds to the reception so that a wider audience would see Jason's beautiful artwork as well as his place in a formidable collection. The commission got made at a loss (*money sacrificed*), but not only was the event a success (*great exposure*), the collector and Jason's relationship and patronage remained intact (*great support*), leading to future commissions (*money in the long run*).

This Book

In the following chapters I will share scenarios that will help you recognize what it means to balance potential gain and compromise against what you're able to change, to forge new pathways. The magic often happens when you focus on the components you can change. I will offer key tools, accessible as part of the ArtSmart Toolkit (p. 20), that allow you to make that change happen.

After we've explored the goals of support, money, and exposure through exercises, tools, and guidance, we'll conclude with the ArtSmart Oracle. This final tool is a way to use the ArtSmart Triangle in your day-to-day decision-making, putting your business autonomy into action right away.

I recognize that the process of introducing new concepts or methodologies that don't neatly fit with your current way of doing things can be jarring—threatening, even. And making career decisions is agonizing. In my experience, artists are so unaccustomed to feeling autonomous or empowered that starting to think this way is the biggest hurdle—but once they've got a taste for it, they're hooked.

The sooner you recognize you're your own best advocate, the better. Wanting a savior to come along and solve all our problems is a very human desire, but it's not going to happen. The gallery is not your savior. Your collaborators are not your saviors.

You'll end up jaded if you hand over responsibility for your dreams, hopes, and wishes to anyone else. This doesn't mean you can't trust or rely on people. What it requires is taking your autonomy seriously so that you're not left feeling helpless and wondering what went wrong.

I want to make sure I'm positioning this book correctly. I've done my best to freely share the tools, exercises, and guidance I've developed over the years to help artists reach business autonomy. There's no replacement for getting to know yourself and your risk threshold through trial and error. I would also be lying if I said that seeking wisdom from either a consultant or a mentor isn't going to help propel you forward. But I truly believe this book contains what you need to start shifting your perspective and start taking yourself and your practice more seriously.

A note to non-US readers: this book is US-centric when it comes to laws and regulations, because that's what I'm able to advise on. But the ArtSmart Method is applicable no matter where you are.

Your creative life can be an organized life. And by organization I mean a compass—a system that allows for everyday peace. This will shape who you are, the art you make, and the mark you leave. To return to the Flaubert quote that we opened with: “Be regular and orderly in your life, so that you may be violent and original in your work.”

ArtSmart Toolkit

The ArtSmart Toolkit is integral to the method. Access it as soon as you can. Use the QR code below, and once you're on the website you can sign up for an ArtSmart account to access the tools and detailed instructions for use.

Each foundational ArtSmart tool addresses a specific need, from networking to budgeting to contracts, and each one has its own introductory section in this book. The tools have been designed to allow you to make informed, strategic decisions about your art—and therefore your life.

Take your time getting to know the tools. They're designed to support you. Play around, try and retry. The risk is low and the potential payoff is big if you can apply even one of them to your practice.

Some of these tools are not unique. Alongside Google Sheets (accessible as OpenDoc, CSV, Excel, and other formats), we've adapted boilerplate legal agreements specifically for the art world. You could easily find variations of some of these online or elsewhere. But the ArtSmart tools are distinct because they've been developed to bring peace of mind to artists.

View the ArtSmart Toolkit online by scanning this QR code, or by visiting artsmartinc.com/artsmartkit

The ArtSmart Method Is ...

... Intended to help artists at all stages of their careers. It's especially useful for those looking to professionalize their practice, or push it to the next level.

... Full of tools and guidance to make informed choices to achieve business autonomy and stop reacting out of fear or uncertainty.

... A way to approach your practice strategically, in line with the ArtSmart Triangle goals of support, money, and exposure.

... Written to be read start to finish first, then accessed when you need a specific exercise, tool, or guidance.

... For people at all levels of business literacy—whether you're deeply familiar with SWOTs or never done a budget.

The ArtSmart Method asks you to scrutinize the beliefs you hold about your practice (and yourself!) so that you can identify what's keeping you stuck.

I will encourage you to empower your thinking and take conscious action. This means pacing yourself and regularly taking stock.

... A way to focus your effort and intention. There is no failsafe route to a successful art career, but embracing your business autonomy can help.

The ArtSmart Triangle

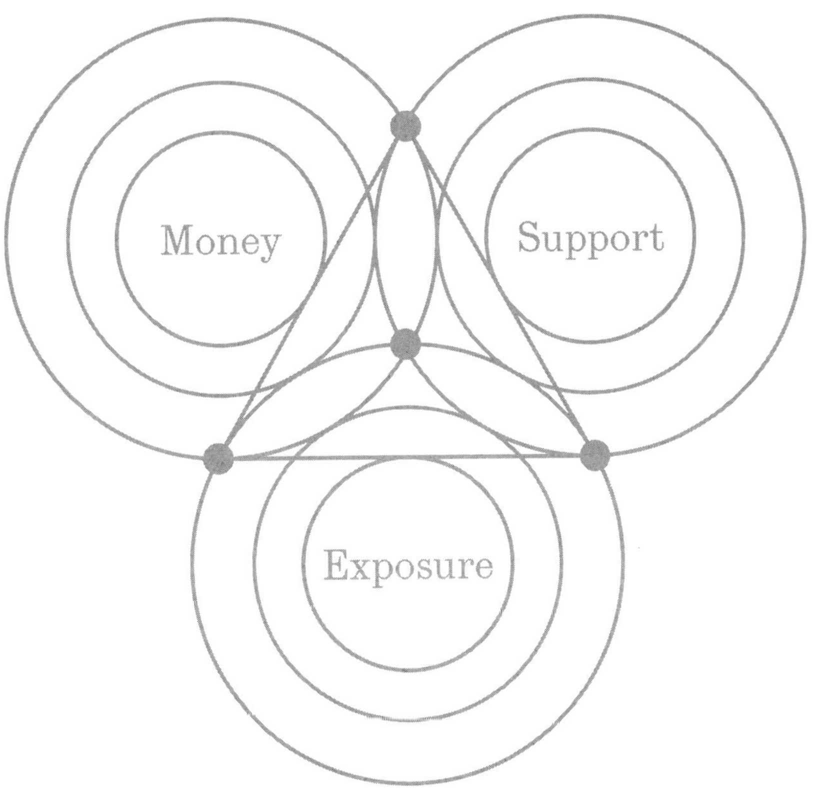
Money
Support
Exposure

01

Plan

10 Questions

You have an idea. It may be fledgling or intricately plotted. This exercise is a way to focus your mind quickly on what you're planning next. It'll give you a snapshot of where you're at in your process, your practice, and what resources you might already have at your disposal. This exercise is a mental warm-up—it's not about instant results.

Paper and pen at the ready—this is one to do by hand.

Look at the below list of ten questions and jot down the first thoughts that come to mind for each. The more spontaneous and unguarded you can be, the better (I'm looking at you, overthinkers and perfectionists).

Don't be afraid to think big. As Gerhard Richter says, "Art is the highest form of hope." Tap into what drives you to create. Reflexivity is key. I recommend doing the exercise in one sitting; some people like to use a timer.

Do this exercise often, and keep your answers. It's great to revisit what you've written at various stages of your life and practice—like a diary of your development and shifting attitudes.

1. Why this idea?
(If "idea" doesn't fit what you're planning, substitute it for something that does: "exhibition," "studio," "series of works," "project"...)
2. Why me?

3. Why now?
4. What other ideas/activities will I need to sacrifice or put on hold?
5. What is the timeline to realize this idea?
6. How many people, if any, do I need to realize this idea?
7. Who is my audience?
8. Where can I share the outcomes of my idea?
9. How will this idea benefit my creative development?
10. How will this idea benefit my professional goals?

Below is an example of a completed 10 Questions. But remember there's no right way to do this exercise.

****

Maya decides she wants to create a series of screen-printed works rather than another series of acrylic paintings. The goal is a new body of work using a new medium, which will require investment in materials and a learning curve.

1. Why this idea?
I gain exposure—which is about impact.

I gain money in the long term, by making a series of prints that can be sold to more people at a lower price point than my paintings. New collector base potential!

2. Why me?
A few people have said they think my paintings would work as screen-prints. I feel like my subject matter—palms and fronds, mythic animals—would translate to screen prints.

3. Why now?
My enthusiasm for acrylic paintings is at a standstill. I need a new challenge. I have a bit of money to invest in tools and materials.

My day job is stable and doesn't take all my mental energy, so I can explore a new medium.

4. What other ideas/activities will I need to sacrifice or put on hold?
I might have to bow out of a group show planned for this year.

I'll need to hold off on any trips to save time and money.

I'll have to sacrifice my painting time for at least this year, which could mean less income from shows and collectors. It's a financial risk in the short term.

5. What is the timeline for this project?
There is a commercially driven art show in early spring next year I'd like to have a space at—that gives me just over 12 months.

6. Who else do I need to realize this idea (if anyone)?
An expert screen-printer—either as part of a course or as a mentor.

7. Who is my audience?
Designers, small boutiques, art fairs, people looking for affordable, unique art for their homes.

8. Where can I share the outcomes of my idea?
As well as the art fairs there is a non-profit Christmas auction for wildlife preservation that I could donate a piece to, in collaboration with the custom framer I use. I can also plan a launch on my Instagram.

9. How will this idea benefit my creative development?
Screen-printing will push me to think about the balance of representation and abstraction in my work.

It'll expand my material and technical knowledge. I can think about working with clothing and textiles.

10. How will this idea benefit my professional goals?

Working in a medium that allows for multiples will sharpen my understanding of how and where to make money from my art.

I will be less dependent on my gallery for income.

ArtSmart PeopleMap

The basic ArtSmart PeopleMap is a visual representation of all your personal and professional connections. Done with consideration and kept up to date, it is one of the most important tools in your kit.

This tool is very popular with my clients. It reminds us that we are all more connected than we think—and that our circle is ever-expandable. This tool isn't just about people in your art life. It's about all the people that you know and have ever known: family, family friends, kids you used to babysit, someone who wrote about your work, a neighbor ... It will help you look at your network with new eyes.

Our connections are one of our greatest assets; most people want to be helpful if they're able. Interestingly, studies have shown that it isn't your close ties that are likely to benefit you most, it's your weak ties that have the greatest impact on your career.

Building an ArtSmart PeopleMap

I suggest filling out the ArtSmart PeopleMap over a few days—keeping it easy to access on your computer will let you come back to it time and again.

To capture as many contacts as possible, think about your closest friends and family, as well as any acquaintances, and professional contacts, then comb through LinkedIn, Facebook, Instagram, the recesses of your mind, and even old digital and paper address books.

Get ready for a voyage of rediscovery (and hidden gems!).

Consider what each connection means to your development. Do they write? Are they a curator you haven't reached out to in a while? Do they work for a bank that has an art collection? Do they build websites? Does their sister run a metal workshop?

You will be using the ArtSmart Triangle goals of support, money, and exposure to establish a key. What you'll end up with is a view of your extended network, strategic alliances, and maybe even where your strengths and weaknesses lie. You might notice that you've got a lot of support potential from your network, but very little money potential—something to think about.

Some people may be helpful in various ways (support and money; money and exposure), but the ArtSmart PeopleMap works best if you identify the most important goal: for instance, your aunt might tell all her art-loving friends about your shows, but it's her municipal government role that can get you an inside scoop on local arts funding.

To be effective, your ArtSmart PeopleMap should be updated regularly—I recommend no less than once a week. Doing this certainly doesn't come naturally to me, so I set a calendar alarm: "Update PeopleMap" every day. Who did I meet at that dinner last night? Who was I just talking about on that Sunday hike? It only takes a couple of minutes, and I've made it a habit. Small disciplines applied consistently over time are what bring success.

Don't skip doing the PeopleMap even if you think you've already done the same thing with a client, collector, or mailing list. This will give you a different view— I promise!

I love this quote from artist and writer Thomas Lawson about not taking people and opportunities for granted: "If I could go back in time and speak to my twenty-three-year-old-self, my advice would be threefold: travel further and more often to see what art actually looks like, figuring out sooner which ideas are currently convincing, which have become passé; spend more time making stuff, less time thinking about it; and do a better job of networking, staying in touch with people who show interest or friendship."

Once you have a fledgling PeopleMap, what action can you take? It's one thing to list who you know, it's another to start reaching out. This can be difficult. So, speak with the trusted folk in your life—family, peers, your cat—to help focus your energy around who to approach and how. Also, have a look at the next section, "The 'Ask'" (p. 40), which offers guidance about approaching different types of people.

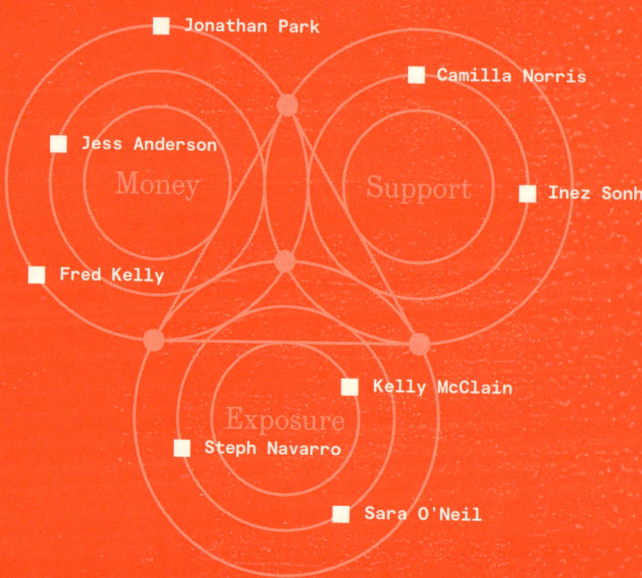

△ Scenario

Off the Street

Kyla was asked to be in a group show at a good museum. The exposure would be vast, but she did not love the exhibition theme. It was about street art, and she was done being relegated to the graffiti camp. She wanted her work to be seen through a different lens.

She didn't want to miss out on the exposure, but equally she didn't want to be misrepresented. She tried but couldn't get any face-time with the busy curator to discuss these concerns.

By filling out her ArtSmart PeopleMap, Kyla realized that she was a few degrees of separation from the exhibition curator. She asked her shared connection to invite the curator for drinks, hoping to broach the subject of the exhibition in a casual setting.

This social meeting gave Kyla the opportunity to invite the curator over for a studio visit. The curator agreed Kyla's new oil paintings sat well with her spray-paint work and with the wider themes of the exhibition.

They agreed that Kyla could include some of her new work in the show. Kyla also suggested a Q&A with the artists at the opening, so she was able to talk about the new direction she was taking, thereby establishing her ambitions in front of her peers and potential collectors.

Our connections are one

of our
greatest
assets.

The "Ask"

Approaching people can feel awkward. Being clear, concise, and having a sense of purpose are the best ways to get people to care—whether they're your best friend or someone you're cold-calling.

You'll develop a personal approach to correspondence, and here are some kickstart pointers. Think about the ArtSmart Triangle goals of support, money, and exposure, and get ready to hone your ask.

How to Write a Professional Email

When it comes to asking for something over email, short and sweet wins the day. The recipient should be able to scan your email quickly and get the gist, unless you're responding in detail to specific queries or requests. And remember, you're a professional who's got something to offer. Ask, don't plead.

Here are the steps to building an email with the "ask."

1. Reinforce your connection to the person and/or their world; remind them who you are. You don't want the email to sound like it was sent by a bot.
2. Pitch your project/idea and explain why it's important/relevant to them. Don't waffle. Apply the brevity rule from the classic elevator pitch—a 20–30 second verbal explanation of your project. For guidance on pitches, I like *The First Minute: How to Start Conversations That Get Results*

by Chris Fenning (2020), and *The Introvert's Edge: How the Quiet and Shy Can Outsell Anyone* by Matthew Pollard (2018). Don't assume your idea can speak for itself or that people will automatically understand why it's something they should care about. If you're struggling to articulate or write out your idea, work with someone who can help you—a friend or a writer you can pay or arrange a service swap with.

3. Ask for something specific—financing, space, access to their network, advice over coffee. Use the ArtSmart Triangle for guidance. Don't be vague; research where they're at and ask for something they might be able to offer.

4. Summarize your email in a gracious and professional way and thank them for their time.

Here's an example. Like most artists, April thought gallery representation was the only way to achieve her goals. To get her where she wanted to be, I needed to shift April's perspective. We built her initial ArtSmart PeopleMap. By categorizing everyone in her life, past and present, April was able to identify possibilities within her network that she hadn't recognized before.

Crucially, while doing the PeopleMap it dawned on April that her day job with a billboard company offered potential for exposure. There were times when they didn't have a client booked for a billboard; April got the idea to propose her work to go up when there was "dead air."

April felt nervous about talking to the owner in person, so she sent an email that allowed her to clearly outline her proposal.

Hi Cassandra,

I realize you're very busy so I didn't want to disrupt your day—I figured this suggestion would be better approached via email.

I've noticed that there are several months in the new year that haven't been booked for five of our billboards and we're getting close to the print deadline.

Rather than leave blank space, I've attached a proposal to place some of my artworks on these billboards. It's a great opportunity to show the city that we're capable of more than advertisements. Also, if artists and galleries—and even government-funded arts programs—saw the amount of exposure they could get, they might pay for their own billboards. This could attract a new client base and revenue stream.

I'd love to know your thoughts on this proposal, and which of the works you think will showcase the billboards in the most appealing way.

Thank you so much for your time and consideration.

Best regards,
April

Her boss went for it, and three of the billboards showcased April's art for three months. By thinking through the connections she already had, she was able to redefine her narrow definition of exposure from something a gallery could give to something that can come in many forms and—more importantly—was in line with where she was in her practice and life.

Here are a few other sample emails using the "ask." The first is to Bill, who is a college peer, and you're hoping he can help you with the goal of exposure.

Hi Bill,

I hope you and Molly are doing well and staying warm this cold winter!

I'm contacting you regarding my upcoming solo exhibition at Prism, which opens on March 3rd. Since graduating from RISD I've been feverishly creating new work and I've shown at various art galleries over the last three years.

For this exhibition I'm showing my mixed media and photography work inspired by my experiences road tripping through the US South last summer. I was fascinated by the nuanced layers of culture that I encountered. The work explores the divisive climate we find ourselves in. I also captured moments of much-needed common ground.

I know you're friends with Natalie at *GoodSweet* magazine, and I was wondering if you wouldn't mind introducing us? I'd love to tell her about the show and see if she's interested in writing a piece or covering it in some capacity. From what she's written about in the past I think she might be interested.

I've included a few images of the work below and attached my artist's statement.

Thank you so much for your time, and I hope to see you at the RISD alumni dinner in June!

Best,
Ariana

For this next one, Jamal is an influencer, and you're looking for his support.

Dear Jamal,

How are you doing? It's Ariana Inness—we talked for a while at the last 4th of July BBQ at Rick and Shelly's. Have you seen them much since? I heard they're off to Barbados for spring break—so jealous!

I'm contacting you regarding my upcoming solo exhibition at Prism opening March 3rd. I remember mentioning to you that I'm working as an artist. Since graduating from RISD three years ago I've been feverishly creating new work and I've shown at various art galleries across the country.

This upcoming exhibition showcases my mixed media and photography work inspired by my experiences road tripping through the US South last summer. I was fascinated by the nuanced layers of culture that I encountered. The work explores the divisive climate we find ourselves in. I also captured moments of much-needed common ground.

I remember that you and I talked about your Instagram presence and your focus on American politics. You mentioned that you have over 50k followers—which is amazing. I've included a few images of the exhibition below and attached my artist's statement. I thought this could be a good fit for your account. Would you be open to posting the show flyer or even one of the images?

Thank you so much for your time, I really appreciate your consideration, and hopefully I will see you at the next holiday BBQ at Rick and Shelly's!

Best,
Ariana

For this last one, Darlene is a former co-worker, and you're hoping she can connect you with her boyfriend and his company for a donation-in-kind.

Hi Darlene!

How's the fashion world treating you these days? I saw your Instagram posts about your new role at Emile Bloch—congratulations!

I'm contacting you regarding my upcoming exhibition at Prism opening March 3rd. I have been feverishly creating new work since graduating from RISD and I've shown at several different galleries across the country. This upcoming exhibition showcases my mixed media and photography work inspired by my experiences road tripping through the US South last summer. I was fascinated by the nuanced layers of culture that I encountered. The work explores the divisive climate we find ourselves in. I also captured moments of much-needed common ground.

I remember you mentioning that your boyfriend Paul works at Capstan Brewery, and I wanted to ask if you think they might be up for donating drinks for the opening night? I'm trying to make the reception memorable, but with funds as tight as they are, I'm looking for some sponsorship. I will happily display a Capstan printout on the drinks table if they choose to donate. If you think they might be interested, I would be grateful if you could connect me with Paul.

Thank you so much for your time and help. I really appreciate your consideration, and look forward to seeing more of your fashion vids on my Instagram feed!

Best,
Ariana

Asking is never easy, no matter how much you steel yourself. Trial and error will always be your best teacher but for more guidance check out Wayne Baker's *All You Have to Do Is Ask: How to Master the Most Important Skill for Success*, Amanda Palmer's *The Art of Asking: How I Learned to Stop Worrying and Let People Help*, and Dale Carnegie's classic *How to Win Friends and Influence People.*

Explore your own emails and think about times when you were approached by people in a way that you found compelling. When did the "Ask" work on you?

SWOT (Strengths, Weaknesses, Opportunities, Threats)

SWOT stands for strengths, weaknesses, opportunities, and threats. It's an excercise straight out of MBA 101 and it's great for when you want to consider a particular project or challenge a development in your work or a response to a proposal or show.

I run this exercise with clients to illuminate what's unique about their idea and to identify blind spots. It's a quick and easy way to poke holes in your plan and make sure it'll still float.

This exercise is the only time I encourage comparing yourself with your peers—otherwise I believe that comparison is a killer. As one my favorite authors Ursula K. Le Guin wisely said, "I'm not competing with all these guys and their empires and territories. I just want to write my stories and dig my own garden."

Bear in mind, the exercise isn't intended to confirm any nagging suspicions that you're a better—or worse—artist than others, but to make sure your work is as robust as possible. A SWOT asks: Is this idea the best way to achieve the result I want? Are there other, better ways to achieve that result?

Copy the questions onto paper, or just take note of your answers. This should be done quickly and with brutal honesty. Your idea about your potential project is likely to develop as you go. You might even come up with something entirely new. For guidance, I've included an example of a completed SWOT (p. 46).

By the way, if your idea is struggling to get recognition because it's provocative or otherwise difficult to position, this isn't necessarily a weakness of the art—you may need to look beyond your current playing field to find support, money, and exposure.

For example, an artist I worked with who had shown in galleries for several years was seeking a collaboration with a toy company for her paintings depicting cartoon characters in the process of decay. She had approached several mainstream companies but they had not responded well to her proposal. By running a SWOT, she was able to recognize that what might be considered a weakness for one type of client was a strength for another.

Together we found a company that was making off-kilter classic toys in line with her own vision. She contacted them cold and built a relationship. The company bought the artist's 2D images to create 3D collectibles, which found a niche fanbase beyond the walls of the gallery.

Parts of a SWOT

Here is some more information on the elements that make up a SWOT and the questions you can ask yourself to develop your own SWOT.

The questions are really just prompts—a starting point. As you get to know this exercise you can adapt them (change, add, remove) to suit your needs. The important thing is to use the SWOT to train yourself to think with critical distance.

Strengths

Strengths are the things that set your idea apart. Strengths can include, but aren't limited to, the medium, process, content, trend-alignment, and uniqueness. It could also be what compelled you to initiate a project. For example, a photographer who makes intimate, large-format black-and-white portraits of youth living on the streets is planning a new series, of smaller-format images. One of the strengths of the work is authenticity. The photographer takes their time getting to know their subjects, and shoots in situ, offering viewers a window on each young person's world.

Ask yourself:

- Which concepts or themes does my idea convey well?
- Which technical, cultural, on-trend, or emotional elements does my idea convey well?
- What would my peers see as the biggest strength of my idea?
- Which tangible assets could my idea bring (funding, gallery attention, customers/clients/commissions, etc.)?
- Which intangible assets, resources, or connections could my idea bring (extending my network, connecting my name with a theme or style, skill development, collaboration potential, etc.)?

Weaknesses

All ideas have weaknesses. As we saw with the example of the artist making alternative cartoon characters, a weakness in one arena might be a strength in another. But before you get into this line of lateral thinking, it's invaluable to put your idea through its paces.

Identifying your weaknesses is arguably more important than affirming your strengths. To continue our example above, because the photographer's work is large format, it can be challenging to find collectors who have the money and space for the work. The photographer has also been doing a similar thing for over a decade and want to look at other format options.

Ask yourself:

- Which concepts or themes does my idea not convey well?
- Which technical, cultural, on-trend, or emotional elements does my idea not convey well?
- What would my peers see as the biggest weakness of my idea?
- Which tangible assets are lacking to realize my idea (funding, gallery attention, customers/clients/commissions, etc.)?
- Which intangible assets, resources, or connections are lacking to realize my idea (extending my network, connecting my name with a theme or style, skill development, collaboration potential, etc.)?

Opportunities

Opportunities are potentialities that you can access to initiate action, growth, or connection. You have to know how to spot opportunities. Sometimes, what looks like an opportunity might be a distraction, or what looks like extra effort or even a threat to your status could be an opportunity ripe for the taking. For our photographer, making smaller-scale work could be a good step. They could post a campaign on Instagram to test their audience's response to their new style. A couple of galleries and a charity have showed interest in seeing a different approach to their work.

Ask yourself:

- Which personal circumstances (financial, psychological) can help me realize this idea?
- Will the cost of commitment be balanced against potential benefits?

- Is there anything my competitors/peers are doing that may positively impact my idea?
- Are there any forces of support, money, or exposure that may help me enact my idea?
- If I'm responding to a proposal, what are the potential benefits inherent in the parameters?

Threats

Threats are external factors that could negatively impact your idea. Some threats, like the activity of your competitors, can be taken into consideration. Others, like a global pandemic or supply chain problems, can't. In either case, threats are always outside your control, but you do have a choice in how to respond to them. Our large-scale photographer may have impact with their work, but their large, expensive pieces may not be resistant to a contracting art market. In the same way that strengths and weaknesses are two sides of the same coin, if you run regular SWOTs, you'll notice that what you perceive as an opportunity or a threat is often about perspective or your desire/ability to pivot.

Ask yourself:

- What personal circumstances (financial, psychological) might impede me from realizing this idea?
- Will the cost of commitment be balanced against potential drawbacks?
- Is there anything my competitors or peers are doing that may negatively impact my idea?
- Are there any forces of support, money, or exposure that will impede me from enacting my idea?
- If I'm responding to a proposal, what are the potential pitfalls inherent in the parameters?

If you're ready for some creative strategization, think about how you can turn potential threats into opportunities. For instance, if a core material you use is suddenly unavailable, should you replace it or use the time to develop other skills, collaborate, etc., until it's available? Or, if a theme that you explore has become popular in gallery shows, should you produce work along those lines, or try something new and push the conversation? We will return to this type of strategic thinking with the ArtSmart Oracle (p. 172).

Here is a sample of a completed SWOT for our large-scale photographer. They are using this exercise to think critically about the idea to use a smaller-scale format for their next series of works.

****

Strengths

Which concepts or themes does my idea convey well?
Social injustice, vulnerability, and strength.

Which technical, cultural, on-trend, or emotional elements does my idea convey well?
Black-and-white, large-scale images allow viewers to get close to my subjects. Due to the housing crisis, youth living on the streets is a common sight and people want to connect.

What would my peers see as the biggest strength of my idea?
Because I was once an unhoused young person, my work feels authentic and raw. I have developed my technical film skills to match the power of these lived experiences.

Which tangible assets could my idea bring (funding, gallery attention, customers/ clients/commissions, etc.)?
Two galleries that have supported my work in the past have been responsive to showing new work in medium format, and maybe even color.

Which intangible assets, resources, or connections could my idea bring (extending

my network, connecting my name with a theme or style, skill development, collaboration potential, etc.)?
Every show I've done has connected me with potential subjects and new supporters. This is a topic that brings people together and I'd be interested to raise even more awareness by making smaller, more affordable work available.

Weaknesses

Which concepts or themes does my idea not convey well?
With my portraits I don't emphasize whether the crisis the person is facing is still happening or was in the past. My work has a strong emotional effect, instead of calling for immediate action.

Which technical, cultural, on-trend, or emotional elements does my idea not convey well?
Each one of my portraits takes a lot of time. I get to know the subject and their environment first-hand. It's also expensive to print the film. This process is not agile.

What would my peers see as the biggest weakness of my idea?
I've been told that black and white can seem like a novelty or crutch. In order to capture the reality of my subjects' lives, I should use color. I don't know if this is true but I think about it.

Which tangible assets are lacking to realize my idea (funding, gallery attention, customers/clients/commissions, etc.)?
I think I'm in a good position with this idea. I could apply for grants that focus on supporting youth at risk, and put in a formal proposal for a gallery show.

Which intangible assets, resources, or connections are lacking to realize my idea (extending my network, connecting my name with a theme or style, skill development, collaboration potential, etc.)?

I'm not known for color or medium-format work. This might throw off some of my supporters, or be considered a bad move. I also don't know how good I'll be at it!

Opportunities

Which personal circumstances (financial, psychological) can help me realize this idea?
I have a great ambition to pivot my practice and expand my collector base. Moneywise, I've got some savings to help me take time to develop.

Will the cost of commitment be balanced against potential benefits?
If I'm able to get a show of my new work, and expand my repertoire, it's absolutely worth the time.

Is there anything my competitors/peers are doing that may positively impact my idea?
I could hit up a couple of the photographers whose work I respect and maybe look at doing a group show or at least getting their advice on how to proceed!

Are there any forces of support, money, or exposure that may help me enact my idea?
One of my collectors from years back lamented that I didn't do smaller works. I could ask her if she might be interested in holding a charity auction for a new series to drum up some exposure.

If I'm responding to a proposal, what are the potential benefits inherent in the parameters?
A youth wellness charity contacted me about a commission for their yearly campaign. I thought it wasn't possible because they wanted color, but I could revisit this opportunity.

Threats

What personal circumstances (financial, psychological) might impede me from realizing this idea?
I'm scared to try a new way of doing things.

What if I spend time and money on it, only to discover I'm no good?

Will the cost of commitment be balanced against potential drawbacks?
I think yes. As much as it's a risk, I fear atrophying in my practice even more.

Is there anything my competitors or peers are doing that may negatively impact my idea?
In this respect I feel relatively secure. My creative community is supportive and shares my concerns about raising awareness for youth in precarity.

Are there any forces of support, money, or exposure that will impede me from enacting my idea?
The market for photography has been shrinking over the past couple of years—but maybe this means it's better for me to use medium format instead of large, so that the costs are lower.

If I'm responding to a proposal, what are the potential pitfalls inherent in the parameters?
I need to get enough practice in this new format before making a proposal or taking on a campaign.

At the end of this SWOT our photographer decided to take the plunge and make a series of medium-format color portraits of youth in poverty. Over the next year they developed their skills through experimentation and working with other photographers. Six months after this SWOT, they ran another one focused on developing a show proposal for a gallery, and another one before contacting the youth charity to do their yearly campaign.

Tackling your finances head on can save

you pain,
frustration, and
hard-earned cash.

ArtSmart Budget

The ArtSmart Budget is a studio or work budget that tracks your production and operating costs. Many people think a budget is about expenses and monitoring spending. But with artists the problem is rarely overspending. A lot of my clients are constantly worried that the sky is falling, so they are cautious to a fault.

A budget is about awareness. It contains data from the past and information about the present to help you predict the future. Budgets are enlightening—I use them immediately on starting work with a new client so they can see in stark relief what it costs to operate their studio every month and where they can tighten their belt. "Did you know you spent $400 on parking last month?" I'll ask a client, before they fall out of their chair.

Tackling your finances head on can save you pain, frustration, and hard-earned cash. There is power in budgets—as we shall see in the coming scenario, they can even help you make transformative decisions. As Willem De Kooning once said, "The trouble with being poor is that it takes up all your time." A budget is a great way to claim back the hours.

Budgets can help with our ArtSmart Triangle goals, too. For example, support is about strategic alliances; you may need to increase your travel budget to meet with key curators at an art fair. By doing a budget you can scope how and when you'll be able to buy a kiln or high-end printer, hire an administrative assistant, or get a bigger studio. You might even see that the money you've spent on a promotional Instagram account hasn't garnered the exposure or support you had hoped.

I encourage you to do a personal budget separately, taking in core expenses like rent/mortgage, groceries, utilities, childcare, student loan payments, and credit card payments and nonessential expenses like dining, gym, charitable contributions, personal care, savings—and pet care. You can do this easily using a spreadsheet program, or there's a tab in the Cost+Benefit Matrix (p. 76) in the ArtSmart Toolkit (you'll need a personal budget to use this tool when we get to it).

Be ready to go through your bank and credit card statements from the last year, catching all monthly costs, like rent and car payments, and all annual costs, such as insurance and subscriptions. Look ahead, too—if you know your studio rent is going to go up next month, for example, include the increase.

Putting time in at the start to get this right will pay off in the future. You'll end up with a financial snapshot that'll hopefully prompt you to consider how you spend your money—which is ultimately about your ambitions and priorities. Revisit your ArtSmart Budget every month to see if you're actually hitting it. Update it in response to reality and to reflect changes in your behavior.

Here are a few examples of the types of costs you can track with the ArtSmart Budget:

Production	Monthly	Yearly
Labor - Production	$ 500.00	$ 6,000.00
Materials	$ 500.00	$ 6,000.00
Merchant Services Fees	$ 50.00	$ 600.00
Research & Development	$ 250.00	$ 3,000.00
Etc.		

Operations	Monthly	Yearly
Auto Expenses	$ 400.00	$ 4,800.00
Office Supplies	$ 35.00	$ 420.00
Telephone	$ 250.00	$ 3,000.00
Website	$ 25.00	$ 300.00
Etc.		

If you'd like to delve further into budgets and personal finances, I recommend two recent titles: Paco de Leon's 2022 book *Finance for the People: Getting a Grip on Your Finances*, and 2021's *How to Adult: Personal Finance for the Real World* by Jake Cousineau.

A Note on Taxes

Taxes merit their own book. My basic advice is to get an accountant or advisor, especially when you're starting out. Otherwise you might miss tax breaks, or end up in hot water—even if you think you're doing everything right (the road to audit hell ...). I'm a licensed paid tax-preparer so I can tell you it's beneficial to have another set of eyes on your books for advice, like be careful of your meals costing way more than your other deductions; payments on principal credit card debt are not tax deductible, but payments on the interest for credit card and business debt are; do not try to deduct personal expenses like groceries or pet care; and make sure to always, no matter what, report all of your income (loans aren't income, but an advance on sales is). The first thing an auditor does is look at money coming into your accounts. Once your art income grows, you should get a bookkeeping program like QuickBooks, or work with a bookkeeper.

△ Scenario

The Devil is in the Details

Caroline is a painter and appeared to have it all. She had a gallery. She had a beautiful studio. She had support from a community of artists around her, money from selling her work without needing a side job, and exposure through modest press and regular shows.

She was grateful, but she was also frustrated that she couldn't figure out how to get to the next level. For her, this meant dealing with a major museum and being included in a biennial or similarly large exhibition. What was preventing her from achieving the success she so badly wanted?

I said we should have a financial planning meeting. She said that finances weren't her problem; what she needed was more exposure. She thought her gallery didn't have enough of a presence in the art world and not enough people knew her work because of it. She thought it was the gallery's problem. I disagreed and said she should be looking at it through the lens of business autonomy. She needed to take charge of her career.

I finally got her attention and we met. We made an ArtSmart Budget looking at the last 12 months. She had made ten paintings and all of them had sold for $20,000 each; half of this had gone to the gallery (the usual percentage) and her take home had been $80,000. We estimated she worked about 3,000 hours in the studio. Her materials, studio rent, utilities, insurance, office, and other expenses came to about $35,000 for the year. This left her with $45,000 before taxes.

Based on 3,000 hours of working, she had made less than minimum wage—a realization that was a huge blow to Caroline. As you go along in your practice, it's good to take a closer look at your budget and see what story it's telling you. The budget analysis gave her some new insight.

Caroline did everything herself. She thought it was more economical than getting someone to help her. But by producing so few paintings she had been limiting her own market. She had also been using precious materials that she couldn't trust to anyone else; they were too expensive. She was completely hamstrung by her practice.

It hadn't occurred to her that if she hired someone to assist her, it would actually allow her to make more work, with the goal of greater exposure and momentum (leading to more money). Doing a budget let her see the situation for what it really was. She had only thought about the money side of the ArtSmart Triangle, without considering how it interacted with the other two sides, support and exposure.

Caroline started using fewer precious materials in many of her pieces, which allowed her to relax in her practice. She also hired two assistants to prep canvases, saving her enough time to double her output for her gallery to sell. The additional exposure eventually led to a major museum acquisition. And it all started with a simple budget.

ArtSmart CashFlow

The ArtSmart CashFlow tool allows you to look at your income and budget and make sure you don't get caught off guard.

The ArtSmart CashFlow, which is in your toolkit, lets you look at current stability, future potential, and old obligations—helping you take the lead in the dance of support, money, and exposure. I often take this tool for granted until I see an artist's shoulders start to relax as we figure out that, no, their student loan repayment isn't going to swallow them up. What you get is real-time analytics, showing you where you can pivot with the current funds you have available. You'll also be able to see when you might be in danger of running out of money.

While a budget is relatively static, the ArtSmart CashFlow shows you how quickly you're burning money over a specific period, taking the inconsistent income of most artists into account, as well as the reality of debt and loans, taxes, and unexpected payments.

There are many uses for a cash flow analysis, such as planning to fund an exhibition or deciding how much money you'll need to save to quit your day job. It helps you to ask the question: should I be saving, paying off debt, or expanding my practice?

As we'll see in the section "Paying Back Debt" (p. 74) there are only three ways to deal with deficits—making more money, spending less money, or taking on debt. Looking at your finances in this way rebalances your relationship to money, showing you how you can treat it with care and respect so that it promotes your autonomy.

The ArtSmart CashFlow has its own tab in the ArtSmart Budget. You will be pulling information in from the ArtSmart Budget so ensure it's up to date. You will also need a personal budget, or at least a note of your total available savings, and your estimated income for the coming year.

Here's an example of the type of projection you can make with the CashFlow tool:

	January	February
Sales	$ 10,000.00	
Total Cost of Goods Sold	$ (1,375.00)	$ (1,375.00)
Total Operating Expenses	$ (9,635.00)	$ (9,635.00)
Net Operating Profit	$ (1,010.00)	$ (11,010.00)
Cash Beginning Balance	$ 50,000.00	$ 43,490.00
Profit/(Loss) for Period	$ (1,010.00)	$ (11,010.00)
Owner's Draw/Personal Expense	$ (5,000.00)	$ (5,000.00)
Personal Taxes Paid - Fed & State		
Loan Payments (Credit card/Term Loan)	$ (500.00)	$ (500.00)
Cash Ending Balance	$ 43,490.00	$ 26,980.00

△ Scenario

From the Past

Drew is an installation artist who had claimed bankruptcy five years previously. Then he started to make a bit of money selling his paintings. Out of the blue he was contacted by the State of Florida, who informed him that his bankruptcy settlement was no longer valid and he was going to have to start paying a hefty chunk of money each month to cover his old debt. He couldn't sleep at night, let alone move forward in finding money, support, and exposure; he needed to reconcile these obligations from his past. It looked like the new payments would force him to decide between funding his studio practice and paying his rent. Because he made large-scale works, transferring his studio to his home was not an option.

After processing his initial dread, Drew and I calmly looked at the numbers. We updated the expenses in his ArtSmart Budget, which carried into the ArtSmart CashFlow. We plugged in his anticipated income (money that was expected to come in over the next 12 months), which allowed him to track how paying off this old debt would impact his cash flow. Not only did he get a vivid picture of what he was facing, he was able to play with the numbers in the tool to see what was feasible in terms of repayment. We worked with various scenarios and negotiated a payment plan for the next 24 months—without leaving him broke or incurring no-payment fees (or worse!).

For Drew, this tool made all the difference because it offered a solid plan—a way to see how he could keep his studio running without losing the roof over his head. Even though his initial projection was based on averages, assumptions, and historical data, he used the tool often as his situation developed, letting the numbers change and staying on top of them. Once he got used to rerunning the numbers and the projections, he was able to get on with his life.

I recommended to Drew that he put as many payments as he could on auto-pay so that they would happen without further consideration. (I can't stress this enough: if payments are fixed, necessary, and consistent, put them on autopay. Why? It preempts the paralysis that having to open bills can bring.) Drew and I figured out that while he was still paying off his debt, eventually he'd be able to save some money, too. That was a great thing to look forward to.

△ Scenario

Quit Your Day Job

Gary wanted to quit his teaching gig, but it was a reliable paycheck each month that he couldn't bring himself to walk away from. We used the ArtSmart Budget and the ArtSmart CashFlow to analyze how much he was spending and how long he needed to work to save up adequate money to feel secure enough to leave teaching.

He lived and worked modestly. He had no outside labor, no debt, and all of his taxes were taken out of his wages. Considering the ArtSmart Triangle, he recognized that he needed a certain amount of financial stability before he could dedicate the time to get more support and exposure.

It's always hard to know what you'll need to feel financially stable enough to take that leap of faith and quit your day job. For Gary, we estimated that if he worked for one more year as a teacher, he would have enough at the end of it to live for a further year without having to make money from anything but his art. He knew that if he just had more studio time he could sell his work and focus foremost on being an artist.

Each month he checked his budget and used the ArtSmart CashFlow to make sure he was on course. Sticking to his guns let Gary quit his job at the end of the year and dedicate more time to his practice, just like he planned.

Rebalance
your relationship
to money ... treat
it with

care and
respect so that
it promotes your
autonomy.

Borrowing

Taking on debt is a serious decision that impacts your lifestyle and freedom to choose. If you get into a situation with debt that you haven't planned for properly, or something goes seriously wrong, it could take years to get back on track. Finding the right financial advisor will help, especially if you're dealing with debt that feels beyond your control. But to avoid ending up in a bad place at all, you can take matters into your own hands. Set a budget (p. 58), do a SWOT (p. 46), get comfortable with cash flow analysis (p. 64), and start a Business Plan Lite (p. 87). These are all free tools and exercises that can save you time and loss.

Once you're ready to seek financial support, make sure it's the right type for you. When I started ArtSmart in 2011, I had very little in savings and knew that I was going to need a business loan. I had no track record, so I looked into start-up loans offered by the Small Business Administration. One program included six months of financial counselling in order to secure a $30,000 loan on a business account from a major bank. During my time in the program, I refined my business plan and developed a budget that included steps to pay back the loan with interest.

The interest rate was 9%, which was medium high at the time, and it had to be paid back within three years. I paid off the loan, but it was a struggle and my business had to stay small. I played it safe for ten years—just me and two part-time freelancers. I couldn't afford payroll, insurance, or even office space.

I survived on a wing and a prayer. With so little capital there was no wiggle room. One mistake, one wrong move, one bad investment, and the whole operation would have been done for. I couldn't expand because I had no way to invest in the business. I knew I needed more money and a longer runway (more time to pay it back) if I was ever going to grow.

I looked at the business through the lens of the ArtSmart Triangle. How could I achieve a bigger support network, a wider market with more access to investment and revenue, and greater exposure with more clients? The answer? A cash infusion. I asked myself if I was ready to take the next step to expand my business. I wrote answers to the 10 Questions (p. 29), and made a budget, a cash flow analysis, and a SWOT. With these in hand I did some soul-searching and decided I was ready. Regular investment in a business is crucial for growth, but your risk tolerance must match any debt you take on. Always seek professional advice from someone who understands the particulars of your situation. Thinking big is one thing, getting in over your head is another.

As a result of the Covid pandemic, small businesses were offered increased access to borrowing. I accepted a $250,000 loan at 3.75%. I have 30 years to pay it back. This amount of capital can do a tremendous amount for a small business, if you have the ability to pay it back. I've been able to hire more people, explore other markets, and make more mistakes—which ultimately led to growth and expansion.

I plotted out how many additional people I could hire and at what rates. I put everyone on payroll, and gave them health insurance and a 401(k) matching retirement plan. I analyzed what new systems we needed to improve, such as data management, security, and internal communications. Once I accepted the loan, I started paying it back well before the grace period for repayment had ended because it was fiscally advantageous to do so.

My own business autonomy story is still unfolding. I have invested, reinvested, borrowed, and reborrowed funds to sustain and grow my business. Scaling up isn't a single move, it's an ongoing process. Every month, every quarter, and every year I rerun my numbers to get a wider picture of the business. Where are the triumphs and failures? How and when should I continue to grow?

What does success mean to me right now? Is it more free time to think and write? Is it more money, a bigger staff and client list? Regularly reviewing my choices and thinking about where I want to be now and go next allows me to focus my energy.

This loan was big for me, and it was a game-changer for my business and the people I employ. But I would not be at peace with accepting this burden without understanding what I was getting into. As we shall see, all money is not created equal.

Debt

Debt is borrowed money, and borrowing has a cost when there's interest on the loan. The costs can vary wildly.

A personal loan from friends or family is likely to be of lower interest or interest-free, but may have emotional strings attached.

Small-business bank loans have varying interest rates and can be lowered if you personally back the debt with an asset, like property. There could also be credit available to buy a particular piece of equipment you need—similar to a car loan, companies will finance large capital asset purchases. Bear in mind that all banks and lenders want financial statements and some will want audits, which means that a certified public accountant (CPA) has verified and signed-off on your statements being accurate and true.

A line of credit is extended for a set amount of time and can be immediately revoked—usually for any reason—by the lender.

Credit cards are often easier to get than bank loans, because they're only looking at your credit rating and revolving debt balance (the amount of debt you're carrying over from month to month).

Equity

Equity gives an investor a percentage of future profits. If someone has invested in you, it may seem like free money, but this is actually the most expensive type of capital you can get for your business—especially if you're successful. You are foregoing part ownership and/or potential long-term profits in exchange for immediate funds. For example, a patron invests $100k in your studio. This isn't a loan whereby the patron would be paid back their principal investment plus interest—they have a stake in the studio and future net revenue.

You must ask yourself if the type of borrowing you're considering reduces your control over the business or project to an uncomfortable degree. Always get someone who understands financial agreements to review potential equity investment opportunities.

Sweat Equity

This type of deferred compensation can take many forms. If someone comes to work for you, but you can't afford to pay them a fair market rate, they may ask for back-end profits, a bonus, or shares in your project or company. The term "sweat equity" is also used to describe a situation in which someone works for free or at a lower pay rate in exchange for equity (percentage ownership) or profit sharing in your business. The key is to have a clear agreement in place.

For example, a studio manager may work at a below-market rate, but at the end of the year, you'll give them a bonus or profit share based on a percentage of net revenue. Sweat equity is also common for artists running a large project—it allows them to incentivize their team for future reward.

Paying Back Debt

When there's a deficit, meaning you're not making enough to meet your regular payments—to individuals or institutions—there are only three ways to deal with it: make more money (take on a part-time job, hire yourself out to other artists); spend less money (close your studio and work out of your home, choose less expensive materials); or go into debt/taking on more debt. That's it.

What's best for you is going to be highly individual. But the sooner you make the necessary decisions, the sooner you can protect yourself from unmanageable debt.

Nobody is coming to save you. Everything has a cost, whether you can see it or not. An investor comes with strings, so does a contract with a new gallery.

Managing your limited resources in a way that keeps you financially safe is business autonomy put to the test.

I would encourage any artist with a new studio, project, or business to aim for the one-third approach to funding. This is one-third savings (your skin in the game), one-third investment (preferably friends and family), and one-third credit or small business loan, or bank line-of-credit with a low interest rate.

ArtSmart Cost+Benefit Matrix

This is another classic business tool that I've adapted for artists. If you want to take an unemotional look at combinations of effort, cost, and revenue generation, the ArtSmart Cost+Benefit Matrix (ACBM) is the way to do it. The ACBM, which you'll find in the toolkit, is not about making work based solely on creative ambitions, it's about making choices based on the outcomes of different combinations of your goods in the market.

The ACBM factors the revenue, production costs, and expenses or overheads of your personal life and studio. It's a satisfying—and truly empowering—way to play with the quantity, production costs, and sales potential of different types of output to see the projected outcome variations of your choices.

I find it has two main uses for artists. The first is choosing a balance between mediums or types of work. For example, the cost and benefit of making five paintings and three drawings for an exhibition, versus making three paintings and five drawings.

You can generate the outcomes of dozens of combinations by tweaking the numbers and letting the tool do its thing. You can do this while planning a series or show, or even in real time. For instance, if 80% of one series is selling on your website and 20% of another series is selling, you can see the financial implications of changing your production line to reflect market demand.

The other main use for this tool is in figuring out how to balance work you do solely for income with your art practice.

Building an ACBM

You'll need your completed ArtSmart Budget on hand and a personal budget/list of monthly personal costs as well.

You'll also need the estimated production costs for the type of work you're analyzing. For example, the relative costs of painting versus screen printing, or site-specific installation versus video art.

Finally, you'll need the projected revenue for the types of work you're comparing in the matrix. This will include the retail price, buyer discount, and production costs reimbursed by the gallery if there are any. You can base this on previous experience.

Once you get the hang of it, the ACBM is an enjoyable tool that lets you consider all types of scenarios. This forethought is empowering.

Those are the inputs you'll be using for the ACBM:

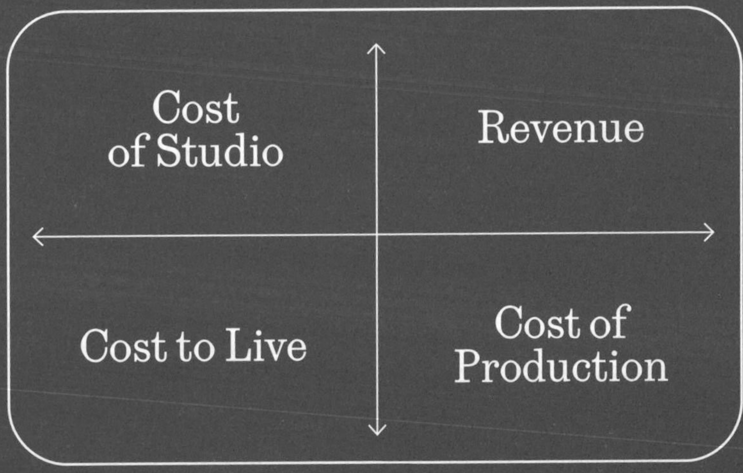

Either/Or

Chen was trying to decide how many paintings versus how many photographs to produce in the coming months. The paintings were cheaper to make, and gained him more revenue, and he had sold 80% of the work at his last show. But the paintings took him twice as long to make as his limited-edition photographs, which cost him more money to produce and retailed for less. But he would get half of his production costs reimbursed by the gallery and they took him less time to make. And 100% of the last series had sold. There were too many factors to rough out on the back of a napkin, so we plugged all the variables into the ACBM, adjusting it with small variations to see how it impacted the bottom line.

The paintings retailed at $20,000 per work, and Chen would get 50% of those profits. Each painting cost him $2,000 to make in time and materials. The photographs retailed at $12,500 and the photographs cost him $5,000 to make, but he received 50% reimbursement from the gallery. We estimated based on historical sales what each body of work would fetch.

Chen had about $60,000 in the bank. It cost him on average $4,000 per month to live and $2,000 each month to run his studio. But his production costs varied depending on what he made and how many works he produced.

He knew that even if the gallery sold works immediately, it would take 60 days for him to see that money, so he needed to be sure he could make his savings last while he waited for revenue. It was a delicate balance of producing works that made him money, and not running out of money while making those works.

The ACBM allowed Chen to see that he had to be conservative in the early months of the year. Then, as he was set to gain more revenue through sales, he would be able to produce more works in varying combinations.

After playing with the numbers, the results revealed that, given his lack of early year revenue, Chen was better off waiting until later in the year to produce a new series of photographs. He also started to think about how he could reduce his production costs for making photos. Playing with the numbers let him map out his production schedule for the year and speak with his gallery about show opportunities based on what he could produce and when.

△ Scenario

Pots Panning Out

June runs a thriving business as a medium-scale kitchenware pottery manufacturer and is also a sculptor of one-off pieces. She wanted to figure out how to think about her time, money, and other resources in order to balance her cash-driven work with her fine art practice.

June has $150,000 in a savings account. She has a hefty studio overhead with rent and payroll. She also has to fill orders for the pottery of about 100 pieces a month—the current studio maximum. Each bowl costs $15 to make and sells for $50. She keeps 100% of that revenue, as she sells directly to a wholesaler.

Her large-scale fine art sculptures cost $7,500 to make, and sell for $45,000. She keeps only 50% of that revenue, as she sells through her gallery, but she gets half of the production costs reimbursed. She predicts that she will sell about 65% of the sculptures she makes. She used the ACBM to run the numbers at the maximum that she could possibly produce for both ventures, to see if she had the funds to keep things going.

Looking ahead at a full year of working tirelessly on both the pottery and the sculpture, she saw that she will end up with a little over $100,000.

She plugged various combinations into the ACBM, including reducing the production costs of her sculptures, and what would happen if she invested more in her pottery, and hiring extra labor to make more, offsetting the costs of the sculpture practice. After a few months of running the numbers and looking at possible scenarios, June decided she wanted to scale up her wholesale pottery business for the next 12 months, which would include training a manager who could take over from her the following year—when June would then shift her focus and money to making more sculptures. Looking at different ways to play this out allowed her to schedule these momentous decisions to give her peace of mind.

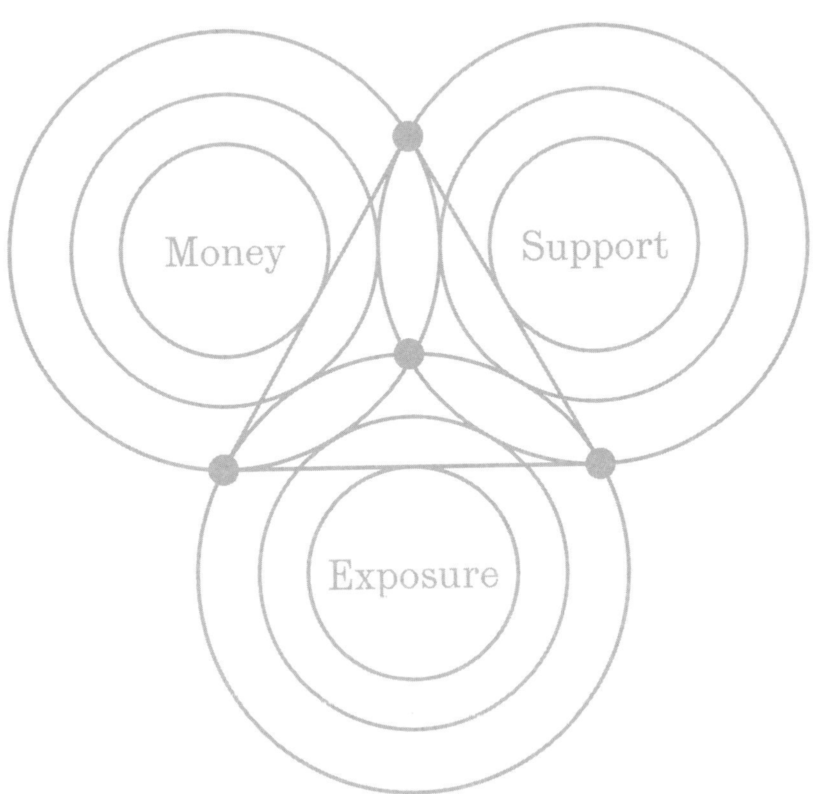
Money
Support
Exposure

02

Operate

Nothing instills confidence like having

the right words at the ready.

Business Plan Lite

Business plans aren't just for businesses. A business plan provides a comprehensive look at every aspect of an idea or project. It is also a deliverable, meaning that if you build it up, you can present a business plan to investors and patrons, for banking relationships, for funding or for institutions giving grants. It's a cheap, compelling way to inspire others to join your project.

I've helped artists establish business plans when they were ready to scale up, for example from one person making ceramic sculptures to a studio of ten employees making commercially available ceramics. Advanced business plans are worthy of their own book.

For our purposes, the Business Plan Lite will let you focus on a current or new business, project, or practice idea. It's good to complete this before registering your business, or even establishing a business bank account. It's an exercise to examine your existing way of doing things, to reflect on where you're at and hone your thinking.

The questions you will be asking yourself here are the same ones you should ask yourself and be able to answer when you're writing a proposal for a grant or commission. But don't wait for an invitation; build your Business Plan Lite so you have it ready when you need it.

While I was teaching on the Sotheby's Art Business Program, a student bestowed on me the distinguished nickname "dream killer" for poking holes in his business idea. I told him that I was applying the same rigor

I'd want someone to apply to anything I had dreamed up, hopefully saving me from years of undue struggle and debt because I hadn't examined my idea from all angles. Instead of killing his dream, I wanted to save him from a nightmare.

How to Make a Business Plan Lite

Most of my clients keep their scribbled answers close to hand (pinned to a corkboard, jotted on a whiteboard) while they're working on it so they can actively revisit it. Over time it should take on your tone of voice and capture the uniqueness of your approach. Keep working until you've knocked out any genericness.

The focus here is not on the creative or existential reasons you make art; it's on how you can position what you do for an audience and for the art market—in a way that feels true to your practice.

To start a Business Plan Lite, ask yourself these two core questions:

1. What is the problem I'm trying to solve? (In market terms this means: What stagnant situation are you trying to fix, or what demand are you trying to meet?)
2. Why is my idea the solution? (What is my unique selling point ((USP))? How does my product, service, idea, or project solve the problem?)

This might seem weird— "Why would I need to solve a problem with my artwork? I make the work because it brings me joy. I make things because I love doing it, not to solve a problem or fill a vacuum," you might say. But remember the ArtSmart Triangle: we're looking at how you can achieve support, money, and exposure—business autonomy.

For example, if you typically create provocative medium-scale collages that are only collected by a handful of buyers and museums, you may want to widen your market.

Problem: A niche market amounting to limited exposure and a ceiling on revenue potential.

Solution: Change the format and adjust the tone for the next two series of works to increase revenue potential and broaden the client base. The new project could be a limited series of smaller-scale, less confrontational, affordable prints.

Get a piece of paper and write down your own problem and proposed solution. Don't worry if it takes you time to get to the solution. Look back at your 10 Questions (p. 29) and SWOT (p. 46) for inspiration (Why me? Why now?), and keep rejigging until it feels like it's snapped into place.

Next, write your answers to the below questions on a piece of paper. It can be notes or bullet points—the most important thing is to get it down. You can formalize and refine it later. I've included an example of a completed Business Plan Lite (p. 87).

> 1. Value proposition (this can also be used as your elevator pitch)
> In business, a value proposition is what a company promises a customer with their product or service. It's got to be short and sweet. For example, Uber's value proposition is, "The smartest way to get around." If we apply the concept in art making, we are looking for what unique experience or characteristics or value an artwork, or series, or project brings to the audience or collector. What's different about it? What makes it interesting and timely?

2. **Key activities**
What you're doing and how it feeds into your value proposition. What gives you a competitive advantage?

3. **Infrastructure**
Who's involved in the organization and how is it structured?

4. **Key partnerships**
Which suppliers, manufacturers, subcontractors, strategic partners, galleries, and collaborators will you work with?

5. **Customers: target market, channels of communication**
Think about where your work has been seen and purchased and/or where you might have potential to expand.

Start making live pitches to people. This can be done anywhere: You're at an opening with friends and the question is asked, "What are you working on?" Try out your pitch as an answer. Keep practicing until it lands right. Before that, hopefully people will ask questions that will allow you to see holes in your thinking.

Nothing instills confidence like having the right words at the ready. Preparation helps you answer the door with confidence when opportunity comes knocking. As the Roman proverb reminds us: "Luck favors the prepared."

For a fascinating look at the "prepared mind," luck, and the creative process, see neurologist James H. Austin's 2003 book *Chase, Chance, and Creativity: The Lucky Art of Novelty* (2nd edition).

Then, Money

The next step is money. Money is everywhere, but the key to accessing it is having a solid plan. For those of you who don't want to wait for a grant or commission or opportunity to present itself, take the initiative. Do further research on how to formalize your business plan. I like the classic 1937 book *Think and Grow Rich*, by Napoleon Hill, and 2009's *Start with Why: How Great Leaders Inspire Everyone to Take Action*, by Simon Sinek.

Here's an example of a Business Plan Lite, completed by Car East, an art duo who make sculptures out of auto parts.

****

1. Value proposition
Constructing the art of Hispanic car culture in East LA.

2. Key activities
Making sculptures out of mangled car parts. The project uses only recycled materials and celebrates the car culture that defines East LA. The use of discarded, forgotten auto parts represents the spirited community that has grown since World War II.

3. People
The team is two native Angelinos: an MFA in sculpture and a part-time art preparator with five years museum and gallery experience.

4. Key partnerships
A local auto body shop that's family run and provides choice parts for very little money in exchange for shout-outs on Instagram.

5. Customers: target market, channels of communication.
We're collected by two museums of local history, a couple of private buyers, and a sculpture park in Scotland.

The auto shop partners have a piece on display. The project's Instagram has 100k followers.

Intellectual Property

How do you establish the right kind of protection for your creations?

Any original thing that you make into a tangible form, including artworks, designs, and pieces of writing, can be considered intellectual property (IP).

Understanding IP isn't just about protecting your own work. It'll help you understand the ways in which rights can impact you more broadly. One of my clients, Patti, understood that it's important to have your work photographed by a professional–it helps with sales and might be the only documentation you have once it goes out into the world. What she didn't realize is that when you hire someone to photograph your work, they retain the copyright of that photograph–unless you lock into a specific agreement wherein a photographer waives their rights (this is not a given). To have the work reproduced you will have to credit the photographer and pay them a licensing fee.

Patti was putting together her catalogue raisonné. She'd kept the names of all the photographers who had shot her work over the years (see Databases, p. 102, for more on documenting this type of information), and so was able to easily contact them to request high-resolution images. She was frustrated, however, that she was asked to pay licensing fees to use these images in the book.

I reminded Patti that photographers were artists too, and a necessary part of the process. Their images showed her work in the best possible light and preserved it. She argued that she had been using these images to promote work, including in exhibition catalogues and on social media and her website. But, I told her, the catalogue was different because she was set to make money from selling this book. It made sense to pay the photographers a licensing fee.

She finally acknowledged that she was lucky to have this problem; these photos had helped her career grow to the point where a retrospective book of her work was now in demand.

The ArtSmart Triangle goals can help when considering IP. By paying money now, Patti was able to get more exposure for her work, and keep good relations with a supportive network of photographers.

There are four ways to protect IP: patents, trademarks, copyrights, and trade secrets. Over the next few pages we're going to focus on copyright and trademarks—the IP protections most commonly used by artists. Copyright protects original work, and a trademark protects things like slogans and logos that distinguish or identify a particular business.

I recommend 2014's *A Surprisingly Interesting Book About Contracts: For Artists & Other Creatives* by Sarah Odenkirk, and 2022's *Legal Guide for the Visual Artist* (6th edition) by Tad Crawford and M. J. Bogatin, to learn more about the legal nuances of IP.

Copyright

Copyright protects original works and exists automatically once an idea is fixed in a tangible medium. Copyright protects your exclusive right to reproduce, distribute, and perform or display the created work, and prevents others from copying or exploiting a creation without the copyright holder's permission. Copyright protects:

- Architecture
- Audio materials
- Movies
- Novels
- Original writing (in other forms)
- Poetry
- Research
- Songs
- Video materials
- Computer software
- Visual artworks

If the original work is preserved in some form, it is protected under copyright automatically upon creation. Things like ideas, discoveries, principles, or a simple list of ingredients (not a recipe) cannot be copyrighted. The timeframe of copyright varies from country to country. In the US, copyright lasts for the life of the creator plus another 70 years (unless another estate or other copyright holder is established).

Works in the public domain, for instance a novel or artwork for which the copyright has expired, or where the copyright has been waived, are free to use. For instance, artworks by Rembrandt are in the public domain and can be duplicated without requesting permission or paying fees to an estate.

To protect your copyright, make sure the work is properly marked with a signature, watermark, or the copyright symbol "©". In the US, you can register your work with the Copyright Office. Officially registering your copyright ensures your work is added to the public record–you're sharing proof of your creation with the world. You will receive a certificate of registration, which makes it much easier to establish a legal case if your IP is used without permission. The non-profit Creative Commons offers free licenses that cover sharing your work under copyright law, with an emphasis on fair, non-commercial public use.

Trademark

A trademark is a form of IP protection that covers words, phrases, symbols, or designs that distinguish a particular brand. A trademark protects brand names, business names, logos, and slogans.

Whereas copyright is generated automatically upon the creation of an original work, a trademark is established through common use of a "mark"—a word, phrase, slogan, or design, or a combination of these elements. You probably only need a trademark if you're setting up a business or brand.

Trademarks do not expire. Trademark rights come from actual use, so if you or your business are using it, then it is still in effect. (If the business closes and you are no longer using it, then it is considered abandoned from a legal perspective.)

You don't have to register a trademark to use it, but it's a good idea to do so, because that will make it much easier to prove it's yours. Also, when searching for a trademark, you'll be able to check whether the business name you've dreamed up is already active. If you're using your name and you see someone else has registered it, get advice from a lawyer that works specifically with artists (California Lawyers for the Arts, or Lawyers for the Creative Arts, for example). Some legal teams and non-profit organizations offer pro-bono advice.

If you're in the US, you can do a trademark search and apply for your own trademark through the US Patent and Trademark Office website. You'll also need to check and register with your state because there's a difference between state and federal trademark registration. Once you're legally set up, you should use a registered trademark symbol "®" to indicate that your property is legally trademarked.

Insurance

As your practice develops and your inventory grows, you might establish a physical studio, start working with people, and negotiating with vendors (galleries, agents). Getting the right type of insurance will help you take important steps to expand your practice into a business. It'll also protect you if something bad happens.

A few years back, one of my clients left a piece of equipment running in his top-floor studio and it caused a flood. Several stories of artists' studios filled with water overnight while no one was there. Everyone in the building, including my client, were renters, and as part of the agreement with the landlord they were required to have renter's insurance. The landlord had never asked for proof, however, so a lot of the artist-renters didn't even know this was a requirement of their lease (always read your lease agreements carefully and ask all your questions before signing!).

The building owner claimed damaged walls and floors, but the artist-renters who did not have insurance could not claim on the damaged contents of their studios. They lost materials, finished and semi-finished works, computer equipment, printers, photography equipment, crates, and more. They also missed out on reimbursement for additional rental space since the studios weren't usable during the clean-up and repair of the building.

If you're on a tight budget and deliberating over getting insurance, thinking about support, money, and exposure will come in handy. If you spend on the right type of insurance, you will receive support from the policy, and will be able to keep working toward more exposure (and hopefully more money in future). Renter's insurance in particular is worth every penny for the peace of mind it brings. If you don't have it already, get it—and talk to the other artists if you work in a studio building to see if they're covered. There'll be less finger-pointing—and more support—if something unforeseen happens and you're all covered.

When looking to buy insurance, bear in mind that, generally, good brokers work for free for you, the buyer, while the insurance companies pay them commission. Avoid fast-talkers and anything that sounds too good to be true. The best brokers are great communicators: responsive and knowledgeable. Make sure they know which insurance companies process claims quickly and pay out without hassle.

Here's a look at the basic types of insurance an artist should consider.

Renter's Insurance

If you rent a space, the landlord will require (but not always check) that you have renter's insurance. This is usually affordable and is necessary for an artist. If, for example, your space gets flooded because of a burst pipe, the landlord's building insurance will cover the cost of fixing the damage and replacing the pipe, but will do nothing when you need to repair equipment and replace supplies, as we saw with the example above. No matter whose fault it is (yours, the landlord's, a neighbor's), renter's insurance is what you need to make sure your stuff is covered.

General Liability/Commercial Policy

A general liability/commercial insurance policy protects your business from financial loss should you be liable for property damage or personal injury caused by your services or business operations. You and/or your business could be responsible for paying various costs, such as medical and legal expenses, as well as compensatory and punitive damages if, for example, a client trips on loose flooring and is injured at your studio. Or if a piece of art made by you or a studio assistant falls off a wall and causes damage to a collector's home, you could be liable. This insurance is affordable and essential to any size operation.

Art Insurance

It's good, but not always necessary, to have art insurance. If you're working with a gallery but storing finished works at your studio, get the gallery to add your studio address as an additional location on their insurance instead of getting your own coverage. If you don't have a gallery, it might be wise to get art insurance in place if you're storing a lot of pieces. A commercial policy or renter's policy will only cover materials and supplies, not completed works.

Art insurance can be costly, so it's important to get a quote at various fair-market or replacement values on your works. Make sure to get a policy that covers work in transit, or add this on when necessary.

The second you start making a piece of

work is when
you should start
cataloging.

Databases

I cannot stress enough how important it is for you to maintain a database of your work and sales. While galleries usually have someone maintaining a database, if you part ways the gallery isn't required to share images or other information with you, such as the names of your buyers. Always ask for high-resolution shots and any relevant information in real time.

The second you start making a piece of work is when you should start cataloging. Your record is the only reference you've got when artwork leaves the studio. In my experience, it's rare to get a second chance to thoroughly document your work once it's out of your hands. Maintain a record yourself—make it part of your regular studio practice.

Each work should be logged with its title, date, medium, dimensions, price, production costs, series, edition, framer, if it was reproduced and where, where it was written about and by who, where it was shown, its market price, how much it sold for after discount, and the amount of any secondary market sales, and who sold it.

Insider Information

I invented the ArtSmart App because I know that having a proper database is key to helping an artist professionalize. There is a demo of the app on the ArtSmart site, but the service is not freely available. It's a big inventory database and management system run by the ArtSmart team so we charge a monthly fee to keep it running. You don't have to use the ArtSmart app to make the method work, but please use some type of database!

Keeping a record of your work helps you organize your thoughts and your studio—offering real peace of mind. (Also, when MoMA comes knocking asking for a retrospective, this database will save your sanity.)

One of my clients, Alex, was in her 70s and had been making paintings and drawings for over 50 years. She had never been represented by a gallery; she'd been quietly selling her work directly to collectors for decades. That was until a curator saw her work at a collector's home and started looking into her oeuvre. Based on this, Alex's work got recognition for influencing a generation of artists, and a prestigious institution came calling about mounting a retrospective.

Alex didn't have a centralized database of where all her sold work was located. Instead, she had a disorganized array of paper invoices, emails, and a few scattershot spreadsheets she'd started and abandoned over the years. She needed to organize all this so the curator could select works, contact collectors, and figure out the costs of the show (loan fees for her work held in public collections, shipping, etc.).

At Alex's request, I waded through box upon box of old invoices and records, and looked through email correspondence and old folders on her computer. I put the information I'd managed to scrape together into the ArtSmart App. We had to locate people to find out if they still owned the work, and if not where it could be found. Needless to say, it took several months to organize 50 years of a working artist's life.

Alex was aware that she was going to gain a tremendous amount of exposure from the retrospective, and support from a new institution and audience, but it was going to cost her money to get all the work organized. Of course she knew it was worth it, and I'm happy to report that the ArtSmart App helped the curator organize an excellent show. But this is also a cautionary tale—if Alex had been keeping track all along she would have had this information at her fingertips, saving time and money, and giving peace of mind.

On a smaller scale, by keeping track of what has sold and to whom, you can get helpful insights. For example, a database will show you whether a collector only buys large or small works. It shows you what discount they've received in the past. It offers the best view of your art out in the wild and your supporters over the years.

Business Legal Entity Setup

Choosing the appropriate legal entity for your art practice is essential because it will have tax, organizational, funding, and liability implications.

It goes without saying that you need to separate your personal and business activities as quickly as possible. Leaving this too long has the potential to create a big, muddy area that will pull you under when it comes to managing revenue and paying taxes.

A "business legal structure" or "business entity" is a government regulation term for an operation that determines your tax burden and liability in relation to your personal assets. There are many different types of business entities, but here we'll be looking at the main ones used by artists and creative businesses: sole proprietorships and limited liability companies (LLCs).

Talk to your peers or a savvy family member, or solicit advice from art businesses that you admire. Get all the information you can before deciding what type of business is right for you. You're also going to want to ask yourself some questions such as:

- What are my business goals over the next five to ten years?
- How much work do I want to do to set up and maintain a business?
- Do I own personal assets that I want to protect?

- Can I afford to pay myself a salary?
- Do I want to run things myself or would I like a partner?

Sole Proprietorship

This is the simplest business entity. If you're an artist working out of your studio with no personal assets that need protecting, like a home, then you can operate through a sole proprietorship.

For this legal entity there is a single owner responsible for all the company's profits, losses, and debts. This is the default mode of operating a business. You and the business are synonymous, so if the business makes a profit, you make a profit, and if the business incurs a debt, you incur that debt.

Setting up a sole proprietorship is easy. There is very little paperwork since you have no partners or executive boards. Contact your local-business government office about setting up business entities in your area.

What a sole proprietorship entails:

- Taxes: Business income is personal income. You are subject to personal tax rates as well as self-employment tax which, in the US, are your Social Security and Medicare contributions. As a sole proprietor you are probably eligible for tax deductions for yourself, your spouse, and dependents.
- Liability: This entity offers no liability protection, which means if the business gets sued, then they could come after your personal assets.
- Costs: These vary by state, but, generally, business license fees and business taxes are the only costs associated with a proprietorship.

Limited Liability Company

An LLC is great if you have personal property to protect. It has a hybrid structure that allows owners, partners, or shareholders to protect themselves personally while enjoying tax and flexibility benefits. Under an LLC, members are shielded from personal liability for the business's debts. The downside is you will be charged state fees and/or taxes even if you don't have any income. Setting up an LLC is more complex than a sole proprietorship, and you should not try to do this without legal advice.

What an LLC entails:

- Taxes: LLCs were created to provide owners with the liability protection that corporations enjoy while allowing pass-through income and losses to go straight to the owners on their individual returns.
- Liability: Owners can limit their legal liability. For instance, if something is damaged at a collector's home by a painting you made falling off the wall, they can sue the LLC, but not you personally.
- Cost: The cost of forming an LLC can range from $20 to $800 for a filing fee in your state.

If you're an LLC, you can opt into S corporation status (this means you become a shareholder in your company). To be an S corporation, the owner(s) must be a US citizen or permanent resident. This status is most useful after you make a certain amount of money because you have to prove that you're able to pay yourself a reasonable salary out of the revenue that your studio business is generating, while still leaving a profit in the company to gain tax benefits. All the money left in the business will be taxed at a corporate rate, which can be much lower than a personal rate. If all your profits are coming to you as income, then S corporation status won't be useful. But if you can live off a fraction of what the studio is taking in, then it makes sense. Bear in mind there are costs to maintaining an S corporation, and strict regulations around inventory and estate planning, so don't get into this blithely.

City, State, and Federal Licenses

If you're a US citizen or resident, in addition to legally registering your business entity you may need specific licenses and permits to operate at the local, state, and federal levels.

In order to do art as a business (and to get a business account at a bank) you'll need three things:

1. Business license (city)
2. State identification (ID) number (state)
3. Federal Employer ID Number or FEIN (federal)

The federal ID is free, but cities and states may charge a fee.

Acquiring a business license isn't difficult, but it's specific to the city you operate in. To be directed to your city's business license website, do an online search for {city name} + {business license} and go to the official site for information on how to register.

You'll also need to go to a state-specific website to apply for your ID number. Do an online search for {your state} + {ID number} to get to your state government's website.

Finally, you are required to have a FEIN (and a state ID number) to open a business checking account, whether you have employees or not. This is federal, so visit the irs.gov website no matter where you are in the country.

Sales Tax Rules for Artists

Tax law is important and the stakes are high. Audits are no fun, and even less so if you haven't tracked your business dealings properly.

For example, you may need to get a seller's permit, issued by the state where you live, which manages how and when you pay taxes on art supplies and other materials, as well as charging sales tax to collectors when you sell your work directly to them, rather than through a gallery.

If you sell work out of your studio directly to a collector, then you must charge sales tax on the invoice if you and the collector live in the same state. If you sell work out of your studio directly to a collector who does not live in the same state, then it is considered an out-of-state sale and you do not have to charge sales tax. (You need to keep the bill of lading (p. 168) to prove that the work was shipped out of state.)

If you sell work to a gallery, art consultant, or broker, they must have a resale certificate, which will include their seller number, which is confirmation that they're allowed to sell and will charge tax when the time comes.

Once you charge sales tax, you are responsible for filing a sales tax return online and paying that sales tax to the state. You might be required to file quarterly or annually, depending on the volume and amount of your sales.

Pricing Your Work

There are many factors to consider when pricing your work for the primary art market: your own historical pricing, size and medium, the cost of materials, the amount of time to make, and fabricator costs, among others.

External factors include the hierarchy of mediums, and what's happening in the art market, for instance if a particular subject or scale is selling well. Whether it's fair or not, the current art market will have something to say about your choice to draw instead of paint, and your choice to make small landscapes instead of big urbanscapes, for example.

An artist I know makes massive drawings that were very labor intensive. They take way more time than her paintings and sculptures, but they can't be priced as high, because the market value for works on paper is usually lower.

Pricing your work high might increase your ability to make money, but it could impact your exposure; some collectors will not be able to afford it. On the flip side, pricing the work too low could stifle your ability to make supportive connections because you'll be too busy in the studio to network effectively.

You want to be competitive within the market without underselling. If your peers are charging $5k for works and you're charging $10k for something similar, you'd better have a good reason that will convince a buyer.

You will often be asked to discount the work at the point of sale (the current industry standard is 10% for private collectors, 20% for large public institutions), while certain institutions will typically ask for a bigger, "prestige" discount because it would be beneficial for you to be in their collection. If a collector or client is buying several works, they will likely ask for a bulk discount.

There are certain collectors who prey on struggling artists. I see no problem selling a few works to the same person, but when a collector wants to buy everything in your studio, you should be wary. Too much inventory in one person's hands can affect the market. For instance, if a collector decides to sell several of your pieces, flooding the secondary/resale market with your work, your primary market could be negatively affected.

It's nearly always the case that everything between the artist and the gallery, or any other consignee (the person or company selling your work), is split 50/50. That means the retail price and the discount are split equally. For example, if a gallery sells your work for $10,000 with a 10% discount, you and the gallery will each receive $4,500 ($10,000 – $1,000 (10% discount) = $9,000/2 = $4,500).

Editions

If you're working with a representative, there might be incentive for them to encourage editions so that there is more to sell. But deciding whether a piece is going to be unique or editioned isn't always a financial choice. I honestly love it when artists make editions, as it allows a bigger audience to access their work. Keith Haring is a perfect example of making art for a wide audience. Along with one-offs, he did editioned prints, as well as badges and T-shirts. Editions can provide income at a fraction of the cost of one-offs. For example, if you spread the cost of a prototype over an edition of 100 instead of one work, the money you've spent has gone toward 100 potential sales, instead of just one.

Production Costs

Production costs include anything related to the making of the work: materials, labor, fabricators, armature, framing, printing, paint, canvas, stretchers.

Unfortunately, most painters to do not get production costs reimbursed. A gallery might front the cost of a canvas for a painter but they will typically treat this as an advance and take the cost out of the final sale price. With sculptors, photographers, and video and multimedia artists, when it's been agreed to share production costs, the split is usually 50/50. Or galleries might even pay for these costs directly and then take their reimbursement off the top of the sale (see the ArtSmart Calculator, p. 152, for more on this).

Be diligent (obsessive!) when tracking your production costs because, even if they're not being covered by a gallery, they are 100% deductible on your taxes. (Don't forget that pencil you bought or that melon you used as a model!)

Production costs should be discussed early on with a gallery, and laid out in a consignment agreement (p. 138). Sometimes galleries will lump other expenses that aren't the artist's responsibility in with their reimbursement sum—for shipping, storage, crating, etc. This isn't necessarily a shady move. I worked in galleries for many years, and people make mistakes. Many areas can be gray or some rules apply to certain artists and not others. It's important for you to double check—you are your best advocate when it comes to getting reimbursed for production costs.

You do not
want to leave
important

relationships
up to a
handshake.

ArtSmart Fabricator Agreement

Your partners need to be reliable to make your art practice successful. A skilled and dependable fabricator—a manufacturer of items or components using tools and raw materials—is one of an artist's most important strategic alliances, especially if you want to create ambitious, complex, or technically specific works that require expert knowledge and handling.

You do not want to leave important relationships up to a handshake. Some people think agreements imply mistrust, but it's the opposite. An agreement says, "I respect your work and our relationship enough to take the time to communicate the terms that suit both of our needs." A robust agreement with a fabricator protects your designs, and the right to use different fabricators in the future.

The ArtSmart Fabricator Agreement is an opportunity to think through potential consequences. As we shall see, if you work with a fabricator who uses special equipment, what happens if you want them to make the same thing for the same price in future? Or what if you want someone else to make the work? These are the types of conversations you should have with your fabricator before the work starts. The ArtSmart Fabricator Agreement is in the toolkit. Here are the terms to include. If a fabricator sends you an agreement, keep an eye out for these.

Names of Parties
Names, company names, addresses of parties to the contract.

Scope
Detailed description of the product being produced, or the work being done.

Cost
Cost of the product or work being done.

Payment Schedule
At which phase of the project or work completion each payment needs to be made and when the initial deposit is due.

Intellectual Property
What part of the IP is owned by the artist and what part is owned by the fabricator. For example, the artist can designate that they own the design of the entire sculpture, and the fabricator, because they designed and used a special tool to make the sculpture, owns the IP of the tool.

Term and Termination of the Agreement
What is the duration of the agreement and how can the agreement be terminated before that time by either party.

Warranties
Assurance that the product or work delivered will be of good quality.

Indemnification
The artist and fabricator indemnify themselves against each other and any third party, for any defects in the product or work unless due to negligence or wrongful acts. This is also known as a "hold harmless" clause—saying that if any defects occur, the person who committed the defect due to negligence will compensate the person who was harmed.

Insurance
Assurance that the fabricator will hold certain levels and types of insurance, like

general liability and worker's compensation, during the agreement.

Limitation of Liability
Neither party will be held liable for any incidental or consequential damage arising from the sale of the product. Incidental damages are costs incurred with a contract breach, e.g. labor costs required to repair something. Consequential damages are a result of a breach in contract, like legal fees incurred in order to fight a party in court.

Confidentiality
Any information such as designs, materials, and intellectual property will remain confidential between the parties.

No Performance
Agreement is based on the work performed and product produced, but there is no guarantee that the work or product will sell.

Force Majeure
If either of the parties cannot perform due to any act of God such as fire, casualty, flood, earthquake, war, strike, lockout, or epidemic, then the party shall give written notice that they cannot complete the contract as set forth. The contract can be renegotiated at that time, or after a certain amount of time the agreement may be terminated.

Dispute Resolution
All disputes that are unresolvable by the parties will enter a nonbinding arbitration to resolve the agreement and terms. Arbitration is like mediation, so it's saying that before a lawsuit happens the parties will enter into mediation with a registered mediator to work things out. Nonbinding means that there will be no court-enforced payment from the losing party.

Signatures of Parties
Signed and dated by the parties involved.

△ Scenario

Agree to Disagree

Cindy was in a bad situation. She had hired a fabricator to build an armature for her sculpture. The fabricator's work was excellent. He had figured out a key issue to stabilize such a precarious, heavy work. She paid him for the job and eventually sold the work. She was preparing her next show and asked for a quote for five more armatures from the fabricator. His prices had tripled since she last worked with him. She could not afford it.

She found another fabricator who said he could do it for the original price she had paid. She hired him, but he was unable to replicate the design of the original fabricator because he didn't have the special tool. But the previous fabricator refused to give Cindy the designs for his armature. In the end she had no choice but pay the old fabricator for the job at triple the cost. The work would have to go up in price too, much to the disappointment of her gallery.

If Cindy had an ArtSmart Fabricator Agreement in place, she could have stipulated that the designs were work for hire, and that would have opened a conversation between her and the fabricator to prenegotiate a price for future work using the special tool. Thinking about the ArtSmart Triangle, tho agreement would have created support between her and the fabricator, and offered her a chance to save money in the long run.

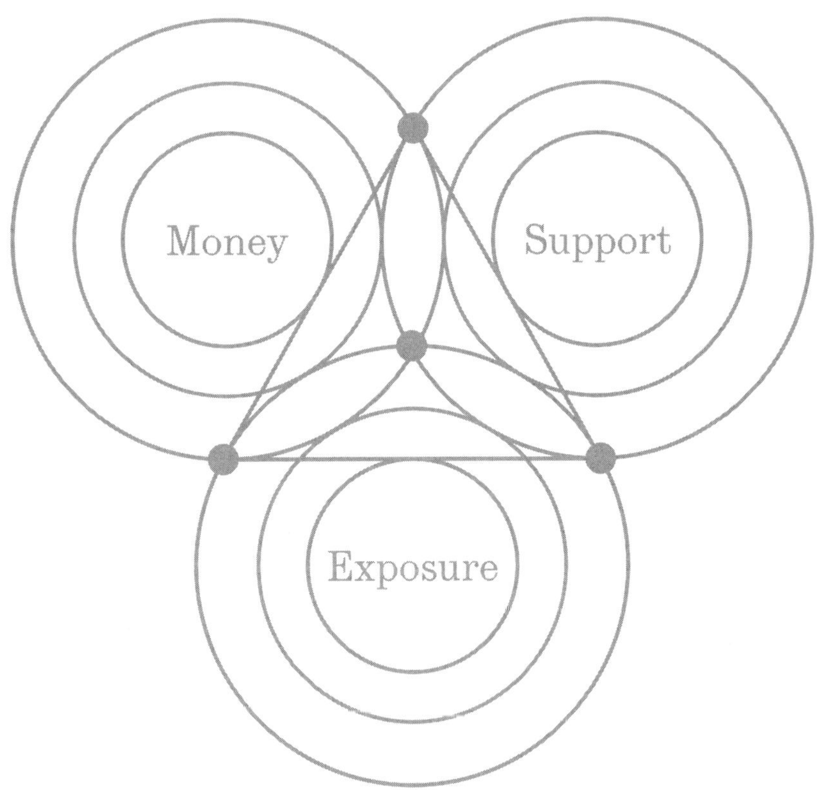
Money
Support
Exposure

Exhibit & Sell

Just because a gallery is hot doesn't

mean it
will represent
you properly.

Choosing a Gallery or Representative

Signing up with the right partner is crucial for getting your products and services in front of the right audience. The reasoning when choosing a gallery should be twofold: their standing in the art world/market and the value alignment with you and your career. Do these two things line up? Just because a gallery is hot doesn't mean it will represent you properly. And just because you like a gallery isn't a reason to work with it.

Timing in finding representation varies. Many artists come out of grad school and see their peers getting picked up. They wonder, why not me? This type of thinking is a downward spiral—focus on what's right for you and avoid comparison at all costs.

Personally, I think an artist should take time to figure out what they want. Think about what they're trying to accomplish before jumping into bed with anybody. If you jump too fast there's potential for things to end badly.

Katharina Grosse once offered this advice. "It's important for young artists to be clear about what they want. When thinking about what galleries they want to work with they need to consider whether they want financial success, comfort, and support, or eventual fame. I look for dealers who challenge me."

When it's time for you to choose a representative, look at your options through the prism of the ArtSmart Triangle. How does this person or institution get you close to your goals? Does this relationship offer you the potential for support, money, and exposure? To what degree and in what combination? Can you live with it?

For example, back when I still worked in galleries, I was hired as a sales director at a new space run by a controversial figure in the art world. My main task was to recruit the right artists to our program. One day during a studio visit, an artist we had our eye on spoke freely about why she was hesitant to get on board. "So this gallery has money," she said. "This gallery has good artists and visibility in the art world. But I don't trust the owner further than I can throw him. I don't want that person talking about my work."

In this scenario, the artist wasn't interested in the immediate goals of money or exposure. What was more important to her was the goal of support—finding an ally that she could trust in the long term.

Connecting with a representative or gallery is a dance. As in any relationship, the courtship is important. Do your research and identify which galleries you like; think how you might fit in with their program; go to their openings and meet the other artists they represent. Put your work forward for auction at fundraising galas; meet curators and arts writers. Thoughtful networking (remember your PeopleMap and the "Ask," pp. 34 and 40) will help you discover who your people are and where they're at. Then you can figure out how to get them over for a studio visit.

Pulling Their Weight

A gallery is probably going to get 50% of your profits, so you need to trust them. For that big a slice of the pie, when they represent you, along with soft skills and selling your work, they should be covering the following costs: installation and display (installers, independent contractor insurance, wall paint); equipment (from projectors to scissor lifts); lighting; shipping and crating; artist, crew, and gallery staff travel; opening and after parties or dinners; high-resolution photography of the work and any events; advertising; cataloging (everything from in-house publications to a commissioned book); and any post-show storage.

Artist-run galleries are still galleries. While they often share more than 50% of the profits, it's likely that you'll have to pay for all your production costs, as well as for shipping and framing.

Personality

You want to figure out whether the gallery owner has the right qualities to make a success of their business—someone you'd want representing your work to other people and advancing your career. For me, the characteristics needed to run a successful business are grit, opportunity seeking, willingness to take risks, and acceptance of assets. This last one is important but needs some explaining. Accepting your assets is about embracing your unique talents and strengths. I know a lot of people who undervalue their own abilities because they reject what comes easily to them. They don't believe it has worth because they aren't in some kind of struggle to make it good. To run a business well, you have to tap into your personal strengths and roll with them.

When meeting an owner, make sure you have a face-to-face conversation in a place where you can focus—a quiet office, your studio, or over coffee in a relaxed setting. See how they communicate: Do their values gel with yours or is something putting you off? How open are they with information? Do they make eye contact? Do they seem trustworthy? Use your instincts, and don't be afraid to ask questions. You've got something to offer—this isn't a hand-out, it's a business deal, so you need make sure it's right for you.

Reputation

Find out what the gallerist or representative did before. Were they a dealer or did they run another gallery? Were they a collector, a curator, an artist? Did they come from an auction house? Why did they become a gallerist or representative? Were they well-regarded in their previous incarnation? How long have they been in this role and at the same gallery? Are they well-regarded now? Who are the owner's friends and colleagues? Are they connected with collectors? What type of collectors? Are they connected with people who run art fairs, with curators, with writers?

One of the most important connections a gallery owner has is with other galleries. Artists often hope that gallery representation will beget more gallery representation. But this doesn't happen randomly. It helps tremendously if your gallery is well-regarded and there is a willingness to make connections in support of your career. It's always a good idea to speak with artists and curators who have worked with the gallerist and collectors who have bought from them.

Team and Communication

The gallery team represents the owner's vision, taste, and leadership qualities. It feels good to work with people who are knowledgeable, competent, committed, and responsive. The team is important because you will be working with them regularly, but your real connection must be with the owner (or someone who has a financial stake in the company).

I recently consulted with an artist who was friends with the gallery manager—so much so that he hadn't spoken to the owner in six months. I cautioned him to get back in touch with the owner even if it was for a coffee—there was no way for him to know how long the manager would be in that role, and he needed to make sure to stay connected.

In the past, many artists wanted to have a close friendship with their gallerist or representative, but that's changing. More and more artists that I work with would rather have a professional working relationship instead of one that's muddied by emotion.

Ultimately, you don't have to want to grab a drink with this person, but you do have to be able to speak with them when necessary.

It's on you to help establish a working line of communication—even if you feel nervous about doing this. It doesn't hurt to straight up ask their preferences: Do they want a monthly phone call or a studio visit every six months? Do they prefer email or meeting in person? Avoid ambiguity.

Program

One of the most important things to look at is the gallery's program, which is the other artists represented. This roster is the signature of the gallery and defines it to the art world. The program will reflect on you and how others will measure and view you and your work.

A gallerist or representative can have the best taste in the world, but if they don't have access to their choice artists it doesn't matter. If the program is already established, you'll be able to see who else is on board, but if it's a new gallery, find out who else has been asked to join and who has confirmed.

Funding

Making money is the single most important thing a gallery does, because if it doesn't, it's not going to be representing and exhibiting artists for long. But there's a delicate balance between making money and placing work. Placing work means selecting the right context, for example a museum collection, or with a prominent private collector. If a gallery has funding (either the owner's savings, a silent partner, or grants) then it can breathe easy and sell strategically. But I think you want your gallery to be a little hungry, so that it gets out there and promotes you.

It's important to look at how a gallery spends its money. I've worked for galleries that threw money around, and I've worked for galleries that were careful with their spending. The latter are still around. The spenders, not so much. Lavish parties are fun, but good lighting on the artworks is more important and indicates business savvy.

My rule is never go with a gallery just because it has money, especially if its structure and reputation aren't going to lead to support and exposure. In the art world it's very difficult to buy these factors. If a gallery has good support and good exposure it probably has a good reputation and so has a fighting chance—and this might lead to money. The opposite is rarely true.

Representation and Exclusivity

If a gallery wants to "represent" you, this is not legally binding. Representation is an informal agreement that either party can walk away from at any point. It can mean that you're on a gallery's website or social media, or that they speak with other gallerists on your behalf or show your work at art fairs. But any binding agreement and its terms should always be primarily about the work—not you or your future career. We'll return to this when we discuss Consignment Agreements (p. 138).

The term "exclusivity" is often used interchangeably with "representation." A lot of the time, exclusivity refers to the parameters of your relationship with the gallery; for instance, you mutually agree that they have exclusive rights to show your work in one geographic location—such as a city or country. It's useful to get this type of agreement in writing (e.g. an email), but a formal exclusivity agreement is not common and should be looked at by a legal eye.

An exclusive relationship with a prestigious partner can elevate your own work or services, but being tied to one partner isn't always ideal. Similarly, be cautious when working with several different representatives; you don't want to saturate the market or cheapen your product. I would recommend not working with more than three galleries at once. It's hard to juggle that many agents unless they're in different markets.

Location

Like a gallery's program, where a gallery is located sets certain expectations. Location reputations can change, so you need to stay on top of what's happening where. For example, in New York, Chelsea has been the home for blue-chip galleries for decades, but these high-profile businesses have started moving into the Lower East Side, which was historically the hot spot for small, up-and-coming, or edgy spaces. The story is the same in most cities: location influences the artists and clientele that will be attracted to a gallery.

A consignment agreement is the single

most important weapon in your arsenal.

ArtSmart Consignment Agreement

The ArtSmart Consignment Agreement is a legal document that grants temporary rights to sell the works listed on your behalf. Like any other consignment agreement, it gives an artist the power to establish the terms of sale of an artwork. It stipulates how your work should be presented, and how you will be compensated. It is your insurance policy against anyone selling the work for less than you have designated, or under circumstance that you wouldn't agree to if you were present at the time of the sale. Whenever work leaves your studio, it should be accompanied by a consignment agreement.

Think of the ArtSmart Consignment Agreement as a prenuptial—you're co-authoring terms that are unequivocally clear. For example, your gallery has a booth at an art fair and it needs to take split-second decisions to make deals. One of these deals comes with a 20% discount on two of your paintings. You have no way of expressing your needs at that moment. But you can "be in the room" with a clause in a consignment agreement that requires the gallery to eat the additional part of a larger discount. Similarly, the gallery can request a clause allowing it to offer a larger discount under specific circumstances—to a prominent collector on the last day of the fair, for instance.

Consignment agreements are likely to get more specific as you develop your practice. You may not understand that your work needs to be shown with a certain type of lighting scheme, for example, until you've had a bad experience. So it's important that you get into the habit early, whether you've been working with a gallery for years or are beginning a new relationship with one; whether it's for a solo or group exhibition or for an art fair; whether you're consigning one piece or 20.

One of the core services I offer is negotiating consignment agreements with galleries on behalf of artists—and I've seen it all. From artists having to pay to have artwork shipped back at their expense if it doesn't sell to artists never seeing unsold work again. I most often see artists wanting to establish a consignment agreement for an existing gallery relationship because they feel like their terms aren't being met.

Often, galleries will send you a consignment agreement. If they do, make sure it contains the terms listed below, as well as any specifics that you want to include. If they don't send you an agreement, you can use the ArtSmart Consignment Agreement in your toolkit and send it to the gallery. If you're worried about what a gallery might think if you make demands, consider the risks of not being upfront and having your work presented badly, or sold in a way that isn't in line with your expectations. You don't have to have an underdog mentality: selling your work is a business agreement and you're the one with the goods.

Consignment Terms

A consignment agreement shows that there are two sides to the artist–representative relationship. It allows for discussion. The artist gets insight into how the gallery operates and its decision-making process, and the gallery gets to see where the artist's priorities and wishes lie.

You, the artist, are the consignor. The gallery or institution to whom you are consigning the works is the consignee. A consignment agreement should contain the following terms:

List of Artworks
Title, date, medium, retail price, your inventory number, and an image of the work.

Time Period of Consignment
A beginning and ending timeframe. This could be exact dates or simply state that the consignment ends a certain number of months after the closing date of an exhibition, for example. It might be in part determined to align with an art fair you would like to show at, or an exhibition at another space that you have coming up for which you'll want access to your work. Or you could also use a simple rule like: always six months after the show or fair closes. The period can go on in perpetuity, and there can be open-ended consignments. But I think there should always be dates, as it allows you to have more control over your inventory.

Commission Split
This is how much money you will get from the proceeds of the sale and how much money the consignee will keep. This is typically 50/50.

Discount Split
This is how much of a discount to a buyer you are willing to split with the gallery. Typically, artists share a 10–15% discount. Anything above that you can stipulate—you either will not share the discount or you would prefer to be consulted before the sale is complete. A gallery can argue for exceptions within specific contexts.

Production Split
Almost every artist incurs expenses associated with making their work. It has become customary that if you track these labor

and material expenses and communicate the information in a timely manner, the gallery will split these costs with you. As mentioned elsewhere, this is usually a 50/50 split (other than for painters!).

Production Cost Reimbursement
This is where you specify when you want production costs to be paid. For example, if you are unable to front the production costs 100%, then specify that once a commitment is made to an exhibition or fair, you will invoice for 50% of the production immediately.

Image Access
Galleries and institutions typically have their exhibitions photographed professionally. You should absolutely take advantage of this free photography and request high-resolution copies for your records.

Photo Credit
When there are printed materials associated with the exhibition, it's important to have your name credited alongside the photograph of the work. The photographer should also be credited.

Collectors and Locations
Stipulate that you would like to know who buys your work and where the work will be located. This is important for your database, for future sales, and future exhibitions, because the prominence of a private collection can help sell your work. If your work is in a museum collection, that's even better. Also, it's important to know where your work is located and who owns it so you can contact them for exhibition loans.

Insurance Coverage
When your work is being consigned, the consignee must insure the artwork "nail to nail." This means that it's completely covered by the consignee's insurance from the time someone comes and picks up the work, through shipment, during the exhibition, through

return shipment, and back to your studio (if the work isn't sold).

Transportation Costs
All costs associated with packing, crating, and shipping the work, including the return shipment, are the responsibility of the consignee.

Damaged Work
This covers who should cover costs to repair a work if necessary, the burden of repairing the work, and who will deem it to be a total loss.

Special Terms
Any and all specifics about how the work is to be shown or sold.

Special Term: Exhibition Specifics
Where the work can be shown (or not shown), for example at a particular art fair.

Special Term: Installation Specifics
If the work is to be displayed in a certain way, with equipment requirements (e.g. projected or on a monitor) or with no other works near it.

Of course, all the above items are negotiable, and each situation will have its own particulars. For example, some galleries may be unable to afford shipping, so you'll have to decide if it's worth doing the show and shouldering that cost.

△ Scenario

London Calling

Kelly was working on a major piece for his Houston-based gallery and was excited that it was going to be shown to a much wider audience at the Frieze London art fair.

He wasn't convinced that a large-scale sculptural installation would sell quickly at an art fair, so he didn't have

high expectations of money. But he was excited about the audience exposure he'd get and the possibilities of extending his international peer network.
When the piece arrived at the gallery in Houston, the owner was overwhelmed by how massive it was and how much it was going to cost to crate and send to London.

There had been a communication breakdown. The gallery owner had been too busy to check in with Kelly or go to his studio. Simultaneously, Kelly had got deep into making the work and it had become something far bigger than he had pitched to the gallery.

The gallery owner knew there was a local collector who was eyeing Kelly's work, so he decided to give her a call. She came in and fell in love with the piece. She was adamant that she didn't want it slipping through her fingers and agreed to pay right away for it to stay in Houston and not be sent to Frieze. The gallerist agreed to make the sale as he was sure that Kelly would be happy to get a check sooner rather than later.

This is a familiar sequence of events. The gallerist felt the pressure—and the opportunity—and decided he had no time under the circumstances to consult Kelly. He believed that if he hesitated, the sale would evaporate. He also believed that Kelly would be excited about the sale.

Kelly was massively disappointed that this signature work wasn't going to show at Frieze, it felt like an opportunity had been missed. Having a consignment agreement in place with the gallery that specifically stated that this piece was earmarked for Frieze would have mitigated this. But Kelly had not made his intentions known. If he'd initiated a clearer line of communication with the gallery, it's likely the owner would have at least consulted him before making the sale.
In the end a much smaller work went to Frieze. It was

sold and Kelly got the money, but the work that he had intended to make a big splash at an international fair never left US soil.

△ Scenario

Breaking Even

Avery was excited about having their second solo exhibition of light art with their current gallery, and they were also certain they wanted to make one major work for the show, rather than several of the smaller pieces they had been making up to then.

They knew the gallery might push back and ask for more saleable works, so they wanted to be upfront about it. They wanted to make a huge impact with one grand piece (a high chance of exposure and support, a low chance of selling). But, based on the production budget, both they and the gallery stood to lose out.

I advised Avery to think strategically. Under the List of Artworks and the Time Period of Consignment clauses in the ArtSmart Consignment Agreement, they agreed with their gallery to consign 20 smaller works that could be sold ahead of the exhibition. These pieces were earmarked in the agreement to cover the production of the large installation.

Because they were proactive and proposed a solution that acknowledged the risk each party was set to take, they were able to get the gallery on board, sell some work and have the exhibition they'd envisioned.

Commission Contracts

A commission contract is a legally binding agreement that defines the scope, deadlines, and money involved in a private or public commissioned artwork or project. A commission contract is for a work that hasn't been created yet. By contrast, a consignment agreement covers a work that already exists.

A commission contract comes into play when you've been approached for a project or work for a specific purpose/place. It's great for when a collector or institution commissions a work that's site-specific. If you aren't offered a commission contract at the start of a project, you should ask for one.

Commission Contract Items

Here's a list of the items you should expect to find in a commission contract. If any of these elements are missing, let the commissioning party know and be sure it gets added. While this type of agreement can't avert disaster, it allows for a softer landing if anything goes wrong. Protect yourself.

Parties Involved

Parties to the agreement are the purchaser, the institution or organization commissioning the work, and the artist and their representative such as a gallery, consultant, or manager.

Description of the Work Being Commissioned

This is usually described briefly in the body of the agreement with reference to an appendix or exhibit that gives a more robust and detailed description of the work, including the title, dimensions, the medium, and special parameters around maintenance and installation. It might also include a drawing, architectural rendering, or images.

Where the Work Will Be Installed or Assembled

If it is a site-specific installation, then this part of the agreement is critical. The agreement must specify the location for the commissioned work and when the site will be accessible for installation.

Each Party's Responsibilities

The artist is responsible for the conception, design, fabrication, delivery, and installation of the work by a particular deadline. The artist is responsible for paying for the fabrication of the work. The purchaser (municipality, private collector, museum) is responsible for paying for the shipping and installation costs. The purchaser is responsible for adhering to the payment schedule set forth in the agreement.

Scope of the Work and Deadlines

The artist is obligated to submit drawings or plans by a certain date, and the purchaser must approve the designs by a certain date. The artist fabricates the work based on the approved designs. The artist agrees to not alter the designs without prior written approval. Once the work is fabricated, the artist submits a detailed plan regarding the assembly and installation of the work, and this is approved by the purchaser.

Waiver of Rights

Once payment is received in full by the artist, the title passes to the purchaser. "Title" is the ownership rights to the work made. So the physical object no longer belongs to the artist. But the underlying copyright still does and always will.

If the integrity of the art is preserved, it can continue to be described as created by the artist. However, once the title is held by the purchaser, the purchasing party may do what they wish with the work—store or relocate it, even destroy it.

Installation Responsibilities

The purchaser is responsible for making sure the site is ready for installation and covers all costs associated with engineering, equipment, crew, insurance, permits, and licenses. These expenses include the the artist's and artist assistants' travel expenses such as the flight, hotel, and meals for the duration of the installation.

Post-installation Maintenance Plan

The artist is responsible for providing a detailed maintenance plan for the artwork's longevity.

Risk of Loss

While the artist is making the work, the artist bears the risk of loss. Risk of loss is if the work gets destroyed due to an accident, such as a fire in the artist's studio. It is then the artist's responsibility to remake the work. When the work is completed, all payments have been received, and the title has passed to the purchaser, the purchaser now bears the burden of insuring the work and the risk of loss, but the artist agrees to take specific measures to ensure the preservation and safety of the work, meaning the artist agrees to make a work that won't fall apart in a week.

Artist's Rights

The purchaser has the right to determine whether repairs or restoration should be made. For example, if the artwork starts to rust, the owner of the work has the right to repair it. Typically, the owner will consult with the artist during a given period about the best method for repairs or restoration. If enough time has passed, the owner may have the repair done without consulting the artist. This period can be determined in the agreement. Some artists want oversight, some don't.

Payment and Timing of Payments

The price for the fabrication of the work is stated, as well as at which phases the payments will be required. Typically, payment is made in two or three phases: the first installment upon signing of the agreement; the second installment upon the final design being approved; and the final payment upon completion of the work before it is shipped. I have seen agreements where a small portion of the final payment is reserved and sent after the full installation has been completed. If at any time a cancellation of the proposal should occur by the purchaser, none of the previous payment installments will be refunded.

Artist's Representations and Warranties

The artist warrants that this is their art, it is original, does not infringe on any copyright or trademark, and that the work was fabricated well. These warranties usually have a time limit set in the agreement. The time limit is specified because, depending on where the work is installed, there may be weather or other environmental conditions that affect it. For example, the work may rust or patina over long periods, but an artist cannot be expected to replace in perpetuity pieces that are getting worn down by the elements.

Extenuating Circumstances

If the artist dies or becomes too ill to complete the work, and the work is at a phase of substantial completion, the purchaser will owe nothing further, and the art to the extent that it is completed will be owned by the purchaser. Things happen that are outside our control. But if the artist doesn't complete the work for reasons other than death or illness, then the purchaser receives a refund. If the work cannot be installed in a timely manner due to the artist's error in fabrication, then the artist, at their own expense, will correct the error.

Relationship of the Parties

The agreement does not deem the artist and purchaser to be in a relationship such as a partnership, a joint venture, or employment. This means that the agreement is a specific relationship between the purchaser and artist and that it is satisfied once the deal is done. The relationship is nothing more than that which is clearly laid out in the agreement.

Notices

Any notices, changes, or modifications after the fact of the signed agreement must be in writing, so that there's no confusion or miscommunication. Emails count. For example, if the work is going to take longer to produce than is specified in the agreement, then that needs to be laid out in writing. If the purchaser wants to cancel the deal, then that needs to be in writing.

Signatures of the Parties

The artist and purchaser sign and date the agreement. If a gallery or representative of the artist is involved and they are party to the agreement, then they also must sign the agreement.

Appendix/Exhibit

This is written by the artist. It is a detailed description of the work, sketches, architectural renderings, images, or site diagrams, including details such as the title of the work, dimensions, the medium, installation requirements, and specifications. The artist should be mindful of sticking to what they have proposed, and that any subsequent modifications should be communicated to the commissioner for approval.

ArtSmart Calculator

The ArtSmart Calculator is in your toolkit, and it allows you to see clearly the breakdown of what a gallery or other seller owes you when there are complex considerations. Mostly, I use the calculator with clients to figure out production cost splits and discount splits.

Confusion often arises because of the language that most galleries use to discuss sales—which doesn't make sense to a lot of artists. A gallery's wording is usually something like, "We will reimburse your production costs off the top of the sale."

"Off the top of the sale" leads artists to believe they're getting 100% of their production costs reimbursed, when in fact they're only getting 50% reimbursed—the industry standard. The ArtSmart Calculator takes the guesswork out of this, so the artist can generate an accurate, professional invoice (p. 156) and have peace of mind that they're getting paid the right amount.

When I worked in galleries, I was constantly meeting with artists who didn't understand their payments; they didn't understand how the math worked—but it's not just artists. Gallery owners would also tell me they were recouping 100% of what was spent on production, which wasn't actually the case. It seemed like everyone was confused—and where there is confusion in the art world, there's room for miscommunication and distrust.

I built the ArtSmart Calculator to show everyone that what's really happening is a 50/50 split. Breaking it down as Math 1 (gallery version) and Math 2 (artist version) makes it clear what's accurate and fair—so nobody has to feel like they're getting a raw deal. Money is the single biggest reason why artists and galleries sever ties. Transparency fosters trust.

Using the ArtSmart Calculator

The ArtSmart Calculator lets you see the sales amount worked out in two different ways. Math 1 is the way the gallery will present it, as a total sum. Math 2 details the splits between the artist and the gallery.

Math 1 and Math 2 should have the same bottom line. If you're ever baffled by a payment you've received, you can plug the numbers into the calculator to be sure you're getting what's owed to you.

Do not rely on a gallery to stay on top of this for you. I've worked for a lot of honest galleries, and I'm a responsible and thorough person, but things can fall between the cracks. The onus is on you to double check the gallery's calculation. The gallery treats itself as a business, and so should you.

Here's an example of the type of breakdown you can expect when using the ArtSmart Calculator:

		Math 1 Gallery Version	Math 2 Artist's Version
Retail		$ 10,000.00	$ 5,000.00
Less Discount	10%	$ (1,000.00)	$ (500.00)
Subtotal		$ 9,000.00	$ 4,500.00
Less production off the top of sale: Gallery prod		$ (2,000.00)	$ (1,000.00)
Less production off the top of sale: Artist prod		$ (1,000.00)	
Subtotal		$ 6,000.00	$ 3,500.00
Percent artist receives	50%	$ 3,000.00	$ 3,500.00
Plus production paid by artist		$ 1,000.00	$ 500.00
Total Due to Artist		$ 4,000.00	$ 4,000.00

Doing the Splits

Missy made a watercolor entitled *Embargo* and it cost her $1,000 in materials. The gallery paid $500 for a frame. The price of the work was set at $5,000. The collector who bought it was given a 10% discount, meaning they took the work home for $4,500.

Math 1 lays out the arithmetic as the gallery sees it. Everyone's production costs are deducted from the $4,500 sale price. So, $4,500 less $500 (gallery), less $1,000 (Missy), leaves a net amount of $3,000, half of which is due to the gallery, and half of which is due to Missy. With that $1,500 for the work, plus the $1,000 Missy fronted in production, it shows she is due $2,500. This is accurate, but could still be confusing.

If we look at Math 2, it shows how the total actually breaks down. So, while Math 1 makes it look like Missy gets $1,000, or 100% of her production costs reimbursed, Math 2 shows that she and the gallery are actually only getting 50% of respective production costs reimbursed. Knowing why she's owed what she's owed puts Missy's mind at ease—and leaves no room for bad blood between her and the gallery.

Missy's totals using the ArtSmart Calculator:

Embargo		Math 1 Gallery Version	Math 2 Artist's Version
Retail		$ 5,000.00	$ 2,500.00
Less Discount	10%	$ (500.00)	$ (250.00)
Subtotal		$ 4,500.00	$ 2,250.00
Less production off the top of sale:			
Gallery prod		$ (500.00)	$ (250.00)
Less production off the top of sale:			
Artist prod		$ (1,000.00)	
Subtotal		$ 3,000.00	$ 2,000.00
Percent artist receives	50%	$ 1,500.00	$ 2,000.00
Plus production paid by artist		$ 1,000.00	$ 500.00
Total Due to Artist		$ 2,500.00	$ 2,500.00

Invoicing

Once your practice is up and running, you'll need to send out invoices to get paid. Even though artists sell different products and services, the components of an invoice are essentially the same for everyone. An invoice is the simplest way to keep track of what you are owed.

Artists who invoice are more likely to get paid the correct amount, including any production costs, or other reimbursements.

One of the artists I worked with during my gallery days earned the nickname Squeaky Wheel. He was adamant about getting paid and would hound me until that happened. The upshot was that I worked harder for him because he never let anything slip, so neither could I.

Meanwhile, a mixed-media artist I know called Donna never wanted to nag galleries about getting paid, fearing that she might come off as annoying or greedy. I wanted her to understand there was a difference between being professional and being annoying. Galleries support you in many ways, but ultimately your business autonomy is your responsibility. It's not about greed, it's about due diligence.

Donna sold a piece as part of a group show in Norway. I convinced her to send an invoice to the gallery and chase it. She used the ArtSmart Calculator to check the payment she was due. She had prenegotiated a split in the production costs that was clearly laid out in the ArtSmart Consignment Agreement.

The gallery was slow to respond but eventually paid her the full sum, confessing they had never been invoiced by an artist before. Also, Donna kept a record of the collector in her database and notified them of her next exhibition, prompting another sale. Like Squeaky Wheel, when she presented herself as deserving of regard, she got it.

How to Draft an Invoice

The invoice goes from you to the gallery. You can send it as soon as you hear about a sale, wait until the show closes, or wait until the gallery has received funds from the collector. I usually suggest asking the gallery when it's best to send an invoice, but confirmation and communication are key. It should match any discount or production costs outlined in your consignment agreement (p. 138).

I suggest checking in 30 days after an invoice is sent, then 60 days after that, or when the show closes—whichever comes first.

If you're sending an invoice directly to a collector, then the payment window is typically 30–60 days.

An invoice shows that you're organized and professional. Always double check your invoices before sending. Triple check, even!

Here are the most common elements of an invoice (some of this is specific to the US):

Full name and address of your company

Tax identification number issued by the Internal Revenue Service
For US residents. This is optional, but saves time when you are asked to fill out a W9 form,

which may happen when you send an invoice to a purchaser.

Full name and address of the client/customer

Date of the invoice

Invoice number

It's important to establish a numbering system that works for your internal tracking. I use the initials of the person I'm invoicing, the year the invoice is issued, then the month or a sequential numbering system for the year. For example: Amy Smith invoiced XYZ Gallery, in 2023 in September, therefore the invoice number is XYZ23.09.1

Ship-to address

If different from the client address above.

Full description and quantity of the products/services being delivered

If it's a sales invoice, it's a good idea to include an image of the work sold. With service invoices, it's best practice to be as detailed as possible. For example, to avoid any confusion about what the payment covers, if you've provided several days-worth of work, or many stages of design, or assisted in a planning process, include the dates the work was done, how many hours, and a clear description of what you did. If your work is outlined in a commission contract, I would include exactly what is stated in that contract.

Price of the goods/services

This might be a flat rate, a negotiated price for a piece of work, or an hourly rate for services. For example, "Edition 1/5: $1,000," or "Phase I design of sculpture and armature completed and delivered on 5/1/2023: $5,000," or "100 × Comic Books, $25 each: $2,500."

Tax

In the US, art is taxable but services are not. If you're invoicing a gallery that has a resale certificate, no tax is charged because the art has been sold to a collector who has paid the sales tax.

Payment methods

This is banking information, which should include: name of the beneficiary; name on the checking or savings account; name of the bank; bank address; bank account number (or IBAN—International Banking Account Number); routing or SWIFT code—this code is provided by the bank and identifies it. You can also list your accepted forms of payment, e.g. credit card, Venmo, PayPal, Zelle, or ACH. I also request that the purchaser references the invoice number when they make the payment.

Additional terms of the sale

For example, a right of first refusal upon reselling the work, or a clause stipulating the title does not pass until payment is received in full. Right of first refusal asks the purchaser to offer the work back to the seller (you in this case) before they offer it to someone else for sale. It's not legally binding, but many artists and galleries include this in their invoices because it lets the purchaser know they can sell the work back in future rather than sending it to auction.

Artist Statements

An artist statement goes from the gallery to the artist upon payment (not to be confused with the other type of artist statement, which outlines the intentions and qualities of your work). The elements in an artist statement should be the same as what was included in your consignment agreement and invoice, but it should also include the name of the purchaser/collector of the work and their location.

Double check that additional items haven't been taken out of your proceeds for the sale, like storage, shipping, crating, or a larger discount than was agreed.

Always save any documents you get from a gallery/consignee. Keep track in a database (p. 102) of what's sold, to whom, and for what price and discount.

An artist shouldn’t issue a certificate of

authenticity
until they've
been paid...

ArtSmart Certificate of Authenticity

A certificate of authenticity can offer peace of mind to an artist and collector at the end of a sale. This is a document issued by your studio on letterheaded paper (if you haven't had a letterhead designed, do it!). It looks very similar to an invoice. It contains the details of the piece, usually an image and any detailed instructions about the artwork, the artist's signature, the artist's wishes on installation, and specifications and/or limitations on how the work should be displayed. For example, if the work is a digital projection installation, the artist can stipulate that the collector should not loan it to more than one place at a time.

An artist shouldn't issue a certificate of authenticity until they've been paid by the gallery, institution, or collector. While it's not legally binding, it provides extra validation for maintaining the integrity of the work.

Historically, certificates of authenticity were issued mostly for editions, photographs, installations, sculptures, and digital works because they can't be signed in a traditional way, or might be multiples, or there may be conditions for how the work is presented. It might also stipulate the artist's copyright over the work. Certificates of authenticity have also been used when there's no "there" there, meaning there is no tangible exchange between the artist and collector. For example, Sol Lewitt's instructions from the artist to the collector indicating how the lines are to be installed, what materials to use, and what colors are allowed. The certificate, signed by the artist, provides the only validation that this is an authentic Sol Lewitt piece.

Certificates of authenticity can be used by the artist to assert their right to payment. I've seen instances where an artist doesn't get paid by their gallery, or is paid but only after a significant delay. In this instance the artist can hold back a certificate of authenticity until they see the money that they're owed. If that same artwork at some point gets authenticated by an outside appraiser, they will ask about the certificate of authenticity. If other works in that artist's oeuvre have certificates and this one doesn't, then the authenticity of that piece might be called into question.

These days, certificates of authenticity have become more common for all types of artworks. The ArtSmart Certificate of Authenticity, which you will find in the toolkit, adds extra power for getting funds into the artist's hands, and assuring the collector they've bought the real thing.

The ArtSmart Certificate of Authenticity is another way to keep your autonomy, alongside the ArtSmart Consignment Agreement (p. 138), the ArtSmart Calculator (p. 152), and invoicing properly (p. 156). Don't leave this type of validation up to a gallery or representative—ensure certificates are only issued by your studio with your signature. Lot's add a sentence.

Here's an example of the type of information that can be included in your ArtSmart Certificate of Authenticity:

****

Certificate of Authenticity

Kafui Ofori
Untitled, 2022
Ink, silkscreen, and spray paint
on wood overall with base
70 1/2 x 49 x 31 inches
(179.1 x 124.5 x 78.7 cm)
Inv# AS 22.012

This document certifies that the piece of art identified herein was produced by Kafui Ofori. All copyright and reproduction rights are fully retained by the artist.

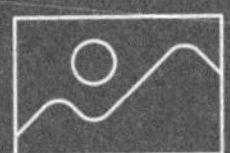

Kafui Ofori

Authenticated Art

Beatrice had been offered an exhibition at a new gallery in Hong Kong and was excited for the opportunity to show work to a new audience. In the past she had shown paintings, but this exhibition was of her photography.

The gallery was incredibly generous. They told her they would pay to print, mount, and frame the work. She handed over all her files but then paranoia crept in. She realized she didn't have a way to protect herself or her work—would it be produced to the right quality and to the agreed amounts? Could she be sure she'd get paid?

No other artists she knew had worked with the gallery; her enthusiasm had got the better of her and now she felt like she was in the dark. Like many artists, she'd been burned before.

What could she do to make herself more secure and be OK with this opportunity? Since she had not put an ArtSmart Consignment Agreement into play, we focused on the ArtSmart Certificate of Authenticity. Each photo would come with installation and presentation details to be sent directly to the collector. We let the gallery know that each collector should receive a signed certificate from the artist's studio as proof of title. We made the certificates on thick paper and presented them in professional, branded folders. The gallery was impressed with the certificates, done to a high standard, and were happy for her to mail them out once she had been paid in full for each sale.

Beatrice sold the show out and was paid on time and in full. And while the gallery proved itself trustworthy, using an ArtSmart Certificate of Authenticity eased her mind and even added value to the final presentation of sale.

Receipt, Release Form, and Bill of Lading

Every time a work is picked up or shipped from your studio, best practice is to issue a receipt, have it signed by the person picking up the work using a release form, and in turn get a bill of lading from the shipper. This will cover you from an insurance and sales tax perspective.

Whereas a receipt is about money, a release form and bill of lading are about the physical work. This exchange of documents will be required if you get audited for sales tax compliance. It's best practice to have these stored for safe keeping and easy retrieval.

Receipt

When a collector, client, or customer purchases a work from you directly and has paid in full, you can issue a receipt. The title for the work then passes to the collector.

A receipt seems inconsequential, but it can be crucial in the event of a tax audit. A super-simple approach is to mark your invoice "paid in full" with the date of payment, and provide a copy to your client (a gallery or private collector, for instance). This can be done digitally or physically. If it's digital, be meticulous about organizing your receipts, or use a digital filing system that is easily searchable.

Release Form

A release form is used when a work physically leaves your studio or storage. It's a way to confirm that, from an insurance perspective, you have handed over responsibility. If a gallery is doing this for you, they will have a system in place wherein they have release forms (and receipts). If it's a sale and you're releasing to a collector, it becomes their responsibility to insure it. If you are releasing to a gallery, but it's still yours in title (i.e. unsold), it's their responsibility to insure it.

Bill of Lading

A bill of lading is issued by a shipper as proof of where that work has gone. In the event of a sales tax audit, you need to be able to prove that you complied with tax guidelines. For example, in California, everything that stays in California with a purchaser/collector must be charged sales tax by whoever is selling it—either the artist directly to the collector, or the gallery to the collector. Once that sales tax is charged, the person that collected the tax (either the artist or the gallery) has to pay that tax to the state. But if the work is sold to a collector who lives in, say, Colorado or Florida, the artist or gallery doesn't have to charge sales tax, as we have already seen. But you can't just fly with the work to another state and show the airline ticket. The only way to prove to the state that goods were shipped out of state is with an official bill of lading from an authorized shipper.

Post-sale

Following up with clients and collectors and establishing a meaningful connection is essential for future opportunities.

Some standard and effective post-sale moves include:

1. Following up with an email to the collector about the work and a personal thank-you note, referring to the work that they have purchased, such as: "Thank you so much for supporting me and my work. I hope you are enjoying the painting *Blue Harmony*."
2. Making sure the collector is added to your database, mailing list, and ArtSmart App if using. Add notes to your database about the collector's interests and what you can offer them in future. Be sure they get an alert about your next exhibition, event, or launch.
3. Follow the collector on Instagram or other platforms.

And, of course, make sure you add the collector to your ArtSmart PeopleMap (p. 34), if you haven't already.

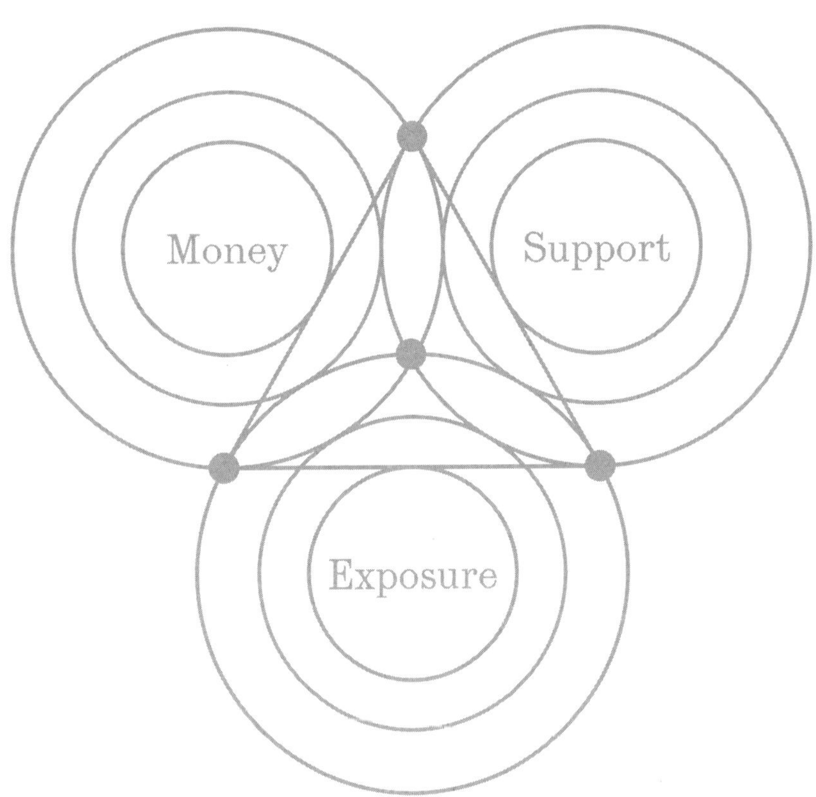
Money
Support
Exposure

Conclusion: The ArtSmart Oracle

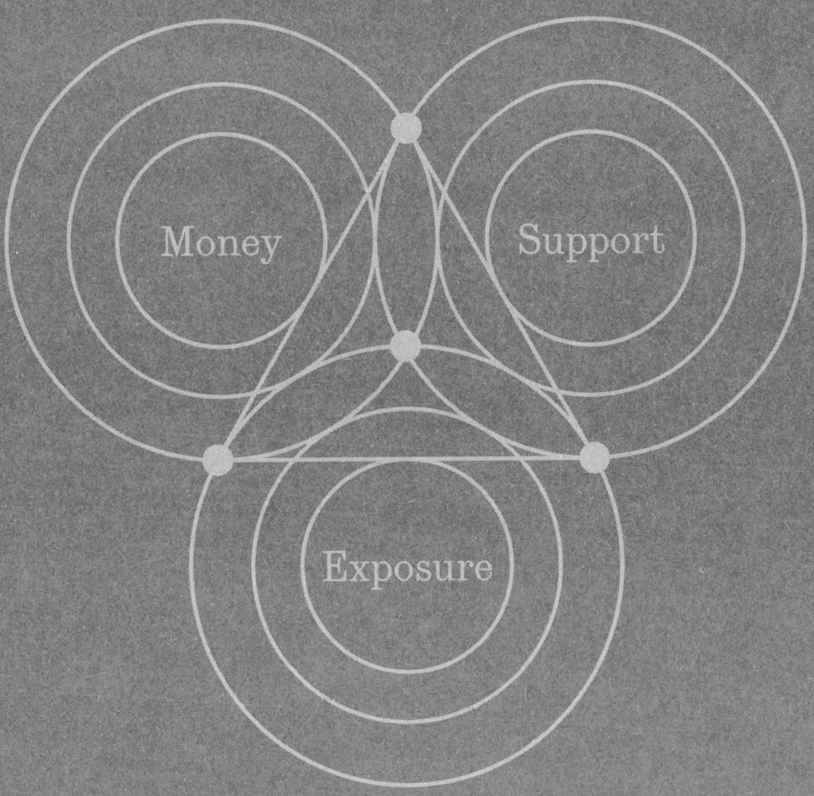
Money
Support
Exposure

It's time to put the ArtSmart Method into

action—with the ArtSmart Oracle.

ArtSmart Oracle

Nobody can predict outcomes. What's round the corner will always surprise you. The way you reach your goals and the form they take may be different from even your best predictions.

Strategic, autonomous thinking can help you forge a path amid uncertainty. Throughout this book I've shown you how to recognize opportunities and maximize potential. By looking at real-life scenarios through the prism of the ArtSmart Triangle, I've emphasized the three goals of support, money, and exposure, which can help guide your planning.

Now that you're familiar with these goals, I want to take it a step further. To make the most of the ArtSmart Triangle, think of each decision—whether it's to spend a month learning a new medium, or investing hundreds of thousands of dollars into a studio property—as an opportunity to recognize and articulate your needs and expectations. You can do this by focusing your energy, negotiating your position, and pivoting to your best advantage.

Organizing your thoughts and actions in this way will help you put your business autonomy first, every time.

Ask yourself:

> What do I want and why do I want it? | *Focus*
> What can I change in this situation? What do I stand to lose? What must I protect? | *Negotiate*

· Have I done what I can to influence the situation in support of my goals? Am I ready to cut my losses if it's not going to work out? | *Pivot*

Knowing when to pivot is probably the most important skill—it'll help you decide when it's time to walk away. Sometimes, rather than solving a problem, it's better to drop the problem entirely.

Divining the Numbers

Now that we're ready to focus, negotiate, and pivot, it's time to put the ArtSmart Method into action—with the ArtSmart Oracle. This is part of your online toolkit. I use the ArtSmart Oracle every day to face life's challenges.

Just like the other tools discussed in this book, the ArtSmart Oracle uses numbers to make projections. It combines known factors with best guesses to help you get a handle on a situation and decide a way forward. In the tradition of the Oracle of Delphi, whose sage words "Know yourself and you will know the universe and its gods" continue to resonate, the ArtSmart Oracle is a conduit; it works best when you look for the answer within.

I based the format of the ArtSmart Oracle on the Magic 8 Ball that I, and maybe some of you, grew up with. This was a hand-sized plastic sphere full of liquid that you'd shake, then peer into its magic eye to see the answer you sought floating in front of you on a small icosahedron-shaped die. If you asked whether your crush liked you, and you were lucky, the Magic 8 Ball would answer: "Without a doubt." If you weren't so lucky you'd get "Very doubtful."

I've morphed this classic invention into something that works with the ArtSmart Triangle goals of support, money, and exposure. To commune with the ArtSmart Oracle, pose your question, then answer either "Yes" or

"No" to each of the four questions asked by the ArtSmart Oracle, about each of the three goals you are trying to achieve. The binary structure requires determined thinking. If you're unsure how to answer a particular question, take a guess and keeping moving!

Remember, money is about financial stability, resources for assistance, funding to run your operation and make your work, abundance for the future, and creative freedom. The emphasis of exposure is on awareness, reaching audiences, and growing at scale. Support is about your team, community, patrons, collectors, wider network, and strategic alliances, and the company you keep.

If your answer is positive, then you score it with a 1. If it's negative, you score it with a 0. (There is no direct correlation between positive and Yes = 1 or negative and No = 0.)

The lowest total score you can end up with is 0, which means you should probably sprint away from whatever situation you're contemplating. The highest score is 12, which means whatever you're being offered is probably worth your time.

THE ARTSMART ORACLE SCALE

12 = Seize this opportunity!
11 = Yes! We love this for you.
10 = This is a solid opportunity.
9 = We like this opportunity.
8 = Most likely Yes, but this opportunity needs some work.
7 = Most likely Yes, but we should enlist some outside help.
6 = Unsure, let's think further about this opportunity.
5 = I see some promise, but we think maybe not.
4 = Most likely it's a No.
3 = Houston, we have a problem.
2 = Not worth your time.
1 = Better luck next time.
0 = Run, don't walk.

Let's look at a few scenarios using the ArtSmart Oracle.

Not My People

An artist is asked to be in a group exhibition at a well-regarded museum. The exposure will be incredible. However, she does not feel it offers support for her work because she doesn't align with the other artists included; they are not her people. The opportunity is positive for exposure but negative for support. What about money? Could this lead to financial support now or in the future? Possibly.

The artist must quantify the likelihood of the show garnering exposure, gaining her financial support now or in the future, and weigh these factors against the downside of the unfavorable positioning of her work.

MONEY FACTOR

Will you make money now? No
Will you make money in the future? Yes
Will it cost you money now? No
Will it cost your money in the future? No

Money Points: 3

EXPOSURE FACTOR

Will you gain exposure to people, or will people gain exposure to your work now? Yes
Will you gain future exposure? Yes
Will this cost you another opportunity now? No
Will this cost you another opportunity in the future? No

Exposure Points: 4

SUPPORT FACTOR

Will this gain you quality connections or relationships now? No
Will this gain you quality connections or relationships in the future? No
Will this damage or cost you connections or relationships now? Yes

Will this damage or cost you connections or relationships in the future? Yes

Support Points: 0

RESULTS

Total Points: 7

Most likely Yes, but we should enlist some outside help.

Analysis: Perhaps there's a way to change the scenario in the artist's favor. While the money factor is still unknown, there is hope because it's a prestigious museum. The artist could encourage the curator of the exhibition to include other artists whose work complement's their own.

△ Scenario

Money for Later

A designer is ready to produce an expensive catalog to showcase his work. It will be a win for support and exposure, but it's more than he's spent before on a publication.

MONEY FACTOR

Will you make money now? No
Will you make money in the future? Yes
Will it cost you money now? Yes
Will it cost your money in the future? No

Money Points: 2

EXPOSURE FACTOR

Will you gain exposure to people, or will people gain exposure to your work now? Yes
Will you gain future exposure? Yes
Will this cost you another opportunity now? No
Will this cost you another opportunity in the future? No

Exposure Points: 4

SUPPORT FACTOR

Will this gain you quality connections or relationships now? Yes
Will this gain you quality connections or relationships in the future? Yes
Will this damage or cost you connections or relationships now? No
Will this damage or cost you connections or relationships in the future? No

Support Points: 4

RESULTS

Total Points: 10

This is a solid opportunity.

Analysis: We have two of three goals in a stable place. The money spent now is an investment in the future, while the catalog itself will encourage exposure. Now he just needs to make sure he gets the best deal possible on the production of the catalog. Vet those vendors!

△ Scenario

Dance Disappointment

A prominent choreographer is asked to collaborate with a luxury brand on its next ad campaign. The money is good but the opportunity doesn't offer support for his work; he's not doing anything that he'd want to share with his audience or even put his name to. But his manager is encouraging him to do it for much-needed funds.

MONEY FACTOR

Will you make money now? Yes
Will you make money in the future? No
Will it cost you money now? No
Will it cost your money in the future? No

Money Points: 3

EXPOSURE FACTOR

Will you gain exposure to people, or will

people gain exposure to your work now? No
Will you gain future exposure? No
Will this cost you another opportunity now? Yes
Will this cost you another opportunity in the future? Yes

Exposure Points: 0

SUPPORT FACTOR

Will this gain you quality connections or relationships now? No
Will this gain you quality connections or relationships in the future? No
Will this damage or cost you connections or relationships now? Yes
Will this damage or cost you connections or relationships in the future? Yes

Support Points: 0

RESULTS

Total Points: 3

Houston, we have a problem.

Analysis: The answer is he shouldn't do it. It makes no sense at this stage of his career to do something only for money—time spent on that will take away from other, better opportunities. Instead, the choreographer and his manager should spend time reaching out to brands that are a good fit for a collaboration.

What's Next?

We've reached the end. I hope you've picked up some insights and knowledge, and discovered a tool that's already changed the way you do things.

What's next? We return to where we started.

The ArtSmart PeopleMap isn't a one-and-done exercise. Add to it often and study it for potential opportunities. Every time you meet a new person, every time you are offered an opportunity, every time you sell a new work, make a note of your new connection. If you're only doing this once a month, start doing it once a week.

Get to know the ArtSmart toolkit backward and forward. Maybe you used the ArtSmart CashFlow tool (p. 64) once, or glanced at the ArtSmart Consignment Agreement (p. 138). Take the time to explore each tool, play with it, and figure out how it can help you achieve business autonomy.

All the tools can be scaled up, so if you've mastered one, see what happens when you extend your range of projection for a longer view—from one year to two, for instance. Using these tools to run your practice as a business can be life-changing—I've witnessed it.

Revisit the exercises. Set reminders to re-answer 10 Questions (p. 29) every six months to see where you're at. Run a SWOT (p. 46) before you embark on any new project or body of work—it'll help you take stock. Take your Business Plan Lite (p. 87) and start a full business plan for your art practice that you can use to get funding or other types of support.

Stay on top of your database (p. 102), whether you're using the ArtSmart App or another program. Dedicating to this level of organization is one of the biggest commitments you can make to yourself and to your art.

Dive in. Be brave.

Reader's Notes

A book by Amy Davila

Edited by Ananda Pellerin

This book was typeset in
BB Modern & Matter Mono.

Atelier Éditions
1545 W Sunset Blvd
Los Angeles, 90026
www.atelier-editions.com

Distributed by
ARTBOOK | D.A.P.
75 Broad Street, Suite 630
New York, New York 10004
artbook.com

For Atelier Éditions
Publisher: Pascale Georgiev
Editor: Ananda Pellerin

Copy-Editor:
Gregor Shepherd

Proofreader:
Rich Cutler, Helius

Designer: Michael Mason

First Edition of 3000
Printed and bound in Mexico by Nocaut on 100% ecological paper from sustainable forests.

ISBN 9781954957091

The author would like to thank her mom and dad for a lifetime of love, support, and encouragement; Isabel for being my moon and Jasper for being my sun; and Ariana for bringing the toolkit to life. She would also like to thank her tireless editor, Ananda Pellerin. The publishers would like to thank artist Matt Schust for his consultations and insights.